D1598939

THE SEVEN WONDERS
OF THE WORLD

THE SEVEN WONDERS
OF THE WORLD

Meditations on the Last Words of Christ

by
GEORGE WILLIAM RUTLER

IGNATIUS PRESS   SAN FRANCISCO

Cover art by Christopher J. Pelicano

© 1993 Ignatius Press, San Francisco
All rights reserved
ISBN 0-89870-417-0
Library of Congress catalogue number 92-71940
Printed in the United States of America

CONTENTS

INTRODUCTION

The Cynic's Blasphemy

There is a proverb of cynics: "If God lived on earth, people would break his windows." Christianity cut out the "if". This monumental attack on a throbbing little conjunction has left cynicism reeling and spiteful. God did live on earth, and people did break his windows. On Good Friday all the words of Christ from the Cross were straightforward, and the only "if" came from the mulling crowd below: "If he is the Christ of God, his Chosen One!" and "If you are the King of the Jews" (Lk 23:35, 37). The speakers assumed he was not, because the facts at their disposal were not the facts they were disposed to accept, and their "if" was cynicism at high decibel.

The Voice of Contradiction knew very well who Jesus was, and so his "if" spoken in the desert earlier was the deadly refinement of cynicism. Satan spat out the plain truth as though it were a cloudy lie. This has been his relentless method: "If you are the Son of God . . ." (Mt 4:3, 6). He says it twice, for the Voice of Opposition turns hymns into taunts.

Satan practically bursts with information he does not like. He was mightily exercised in the three hours of Good Friday because of information he hated: "God was in Christ reconciling the world to himself . . ." (2 Cor 5:19). The agony of Christ was an agony to Satan because Christ endured what Satan tried to prevent. The Passion confused Satan's surgical annihilation of God. That destruction was to have been like the swift work of a lizard with bored eyes darting his tongue at a fly; but the Crucifixion prolonged what hell wanted to be quick and unnoticed by the human race. We must suppose that Satan still cannot forgive Providence for providing an agony that would expose his infernal malice. When our Lord walked on the earth, Satan affected an attitude of mocking condescension toward the Most High who was making himself so low. The same Creed that is the Church's boldest hymn, whether gasped by one old man eaten by a cancer or sung by the silvery choirs of Vivaldi or Bach, was a cynical slur on Satan's sharp tongue: "I know who you are, the Holy One of God" (Mk 1:24).

The Evil One has a way of announcing the Good News as though it were a threatening letter. And there is a threatening element in the news: God did live among men as a man for something more than thirty years, a fragment of time like the melting of a chip of ice compared with the age of the universe, and that brief-lived flesh was broken by whips and thorns and thornier human hands. Not a bone in his body was broken, but nearly everything around him was shattered, from the rent sky and quaked earth to the torn temple veil and fractured consciences of whole mobs making mock genuflections to him.

The profligate horror of it should have branded cynicism onto any smooth logic. Yet since then, cynicism has been a blasphemy. Its Friday is even capitalized as a Good, because its minuscule trinity of hours was willed by the Eternal Trinity. Once you acknowledge that, almost anything else you try to say about it is slightly vulgar. Were we angels, we would be silent on the ramparts. We are a little lower than the angels, and, looking up at the Cross from a human level, we seem clumsy as we crane our necks. Some awkward news broadcasters have been heard wishing Christian listeners a "Happy Good Friday". The fact of God living on earth and the meaning of God's getting his human windows broken start to resonate and then shake unsteadily when one begins to realize that Christ's day on the Cross was not happy and was nevertheless good.

Astonishment

Christ was perfect God and perfect man. God is not vulnerable, not in his eternal self-sufficiency, even when his Second Person is crucified on the Cross. His divine personhood cannot be killed, nor can his divine nature as it was revealed to us in those years of his on earth; his human nature can. God has no blood. The God-Man does. And in the Holy Passion the blood is shed. In the sharpest literal sense this spectacle is wonderful. In a chain of words like a chain of events, a wonder causes astonishment, and to astonish is "to deprive of sensation, as by a blow; to stun, paralyze, deaden, stupefy". That is the line of one arbiter of definitions, the Oxford English Dictionary, and it should suffice to describe what was done physically to Jesus Christ.

He was deprived of sensation by wave upon wave of iron blows, stunned by the affront of it all, paralyzed by nails, deadened by asphyxiation and blood loss and stupefied until his seventh utterance was his last. Or so it seemed for the moment. If he appeared to be astonished, he was not surprised. Surprise is a far different thing. It is the reaction to loss of control. The apparent astonishment of Christ did not come as a surprise, not in any way. Its virulence came to him as a foreboding. It was planned, and his cavernous moral struggle consisted in obeying the plan. "I have set my face like a flint" said the prophet Isaiah when he determined to obey the Lord's plan, and when the Lord himself was determined, "he set his face to go to Jerusalem" (Is

50:7; Lk 9:51). All the valiant scraps theologians can ever say about what they call eschatology will be explained by uncovering what those two passages mean; and everything right theologians read into Christology is written between the lines on Christ's unlined face. For the mystery consists in how the Holy Face faces. After entering the city, when even the Greeks began to seek him out, he turned his face to the heavens and prayed, "Now is my soul troubled. And what shall I say? 'Father, save me from this hour'? No, for this purpose I have come to this hour. Father, glorify thy name" (Jn 12:27–28).

His struggle to follow the course of events as planned was in graceful tandem with his effort to enlist those around him in the unfolding events. Everyone had a part to play in the Passion, even if it was horse-play, for everyone has a part to play in creation. The Passion was the plan to restore creation to its rightful purpose of giving delight to the Creator. "You did not choose me, but I chose you . . ." (Jn 15:16). The words, spoken in a stillness of a rented upper-storey room before his arrest, were spoken quietly. Their solemn tranquillity persists to the present time as no shout could have. It is as defiant as ever now against the shabby modern claims that God is a self-projection and that the boundaries of reality are defined by the human ego.

The Passion of Christ shattered subjectivism. False philosophies today are puzzles put together with pieces from the rubble. This is a most astonishing thing about the Crucifixion, so far as modern philosophical attitudes are concerned. The Son of God is as solid and objective as the Cross to which he was nailed. When he declares that we did not chose him, that he chose us, he says in philosophical idiom: "You did not astonish me, I astonished you." Each of his words from the Cross is a blow harder than a hammer's, striking at the lies that make human pride cogent. The words of the Crucified stun complacency, paralyze defiance, deaden vanity and stupefy arrogance, once human consciences come off the moral painkillers that sloth and scepticism came close to perfecting in modern decades.

The Significance of Signs

Civilization progresses according to its estimation of what makes wonders wonderful. Little wonders do not add up to the large wonder of the Cross. At most they may point to it. What really matters is that they do matter. They "have significance"; and more precisely, they signify the destined "Hour" of Christ. Signs sought for their spectacle apart from their significance can weaken the virtue of faith: "Unless you see signs and wonders you will not believe" (Jn 4:48). And wonders pretending to signify can menace faith: "For false Christs and false prophets will arise and show great signs and wonders, so as to lead astray, if possible, even the elect" (Mt 24:24).

The accounts of Christ's miracles record the reaction to them as an intrinsic part of the theme. All wondered at what the shepherds told them of the angel, and the throng wondered when they saw the dumb speak, the maimed restored, the lame walk and the blind see. But a miracle performed remains a stunt like a fast dance on a platform, until its witnesses begin to understand why it is performed. The disciples were astounded when he walked on the water, and because "their hearts were hardened" they made no connection between this miracle and the miracle of the loaves. They felt confused by something superhuman instead of awed by something supernatural. Those who wondered at his gracious words in the synagogue at Nazareth reacted by trying to throw him off a cliff. His calming of the storm made the

disciples more restless than when the waves were wild.
When he exorcized the Gerasene, the herdsmen fled and the
crowd asked him to leave the area. When he gave a man the
gift of speech, some of those who marvelled called him a
devil. Miracles do not get their message across to personalities dazzled instead of illuminated.

The Working of the Divine Will

Christ's teachings were grasped more directly than his physical signs. The Sermon on the Mount was a string of moral
wonders, not physical, but wondrous nonetheless: "And it
came to pass, when Jesus had ended these sayings, the people
were astonished at his doctrine" (Mt 7:28). For all their nonchalance and even commonplaceness, they gave a razor
sharpness to logic. Judge not, that you be not judged. Do not
give dogs what is holy. Ask, and it will be given you. Enter
by the narrow gate; for the gate is wide and the way is easy
that leads to destruction. Beware of false prophets. Not every
one who says to me "Lord, Lord" shall enter the Kingdom
of heaven but he who does the will of my Father who is in
heaven. Everyone then who hears these words of mine and
does them will be like a wise man who built his house upon
the rock (Mt 7:1ff.).

It takes a divine intelligence to be so matter-of-fact about
facts. The human instinct is to treat radical realities as problematic and, if we are modern enough, to suspect that they
may even be delusions. That was not Christ's way, and no
one had to tell him to come down off his high horse when
he had finished. He simply came down a mountain. And
crowds followed him. It cannot be said that they were
merely dazzled this time. It can be said that their moral fabric had been dealt a deeply moral blow, and their countless

affectations of inhumanity that pride proposes had been stunned and paralyzed.

As soon as he had finished the Sermon on the Mount, a curious thing happened: the physical kind of miracle. For a leper approached him, and rather according to the script for such an encounter he knelt saying, "Lord, if you will, you can make me clean" (Mt 8:2; cf. Mk 1:40; Lk 5:12). When the leper was healed, it would have been easy to be distracted from the moral power of the sermon just preached. But the physical sign is very much part of the moral drama that will culminate in the "Hour" of the Passion. For when Christ stretched out his hand and touched the leper, he said, "I will."

The healing of the leper was a feeble incident compared with the depth and age of that utterance and an irrelevancy if separated from it. The whole universe came into being by the power of that same utterance. "I will." And by submitting to the moral force of that same will, Mary of Nazareth consented for the divine will to take flesh in his world. In a Muslim tradition, eclectically living off true revelation, the Blessed Virgin explains to Joseph the miraculous birth of her Son: "Do you not know that God when he created the wheat had no need of seed, and that God by his power made the trees without the help of rain? All that God had to do was to say 'So be it', and it was done."

To question whether God made the world is a mechanical way of asking whether God willed the world. But the nature of human being shapes the question "Did God make us?" and makes it almost unnatural to ask "Did God will us?" Humans have the ability to make certain things, because they have been made by Another, and their creations are essentially procreations. We create by acting. But humans do not have the ability to create by willing. That is the unique property of God, who is perfect Being. A "human being" survives only as a "human doing". This is why, in the case of humans, "How are you?" and "How do you do?" mean the same. But in the case of God Almighty, the inquirers ask how can he possibly be, and the believers pray "Our Father who art", but no one has the absence of mind to ask him "How do you do?" Even the rare "human doers" known as "wonder-workers" are not wonder-makers; if they do perform miracles, these are by divine will, and the workers of them are agents. No intensity of interior vigilance can of itself make a wish a fact. Saints perform miracles, but the miracles do not prove their sanctity. The evidence of sanctity is heroic virtue, and only within a life of such virtue is a miraculous display a sign of heaven itself.

Cataloguing the Wonders

Man left to himself can at best imitate the miraculous by simulating its ability to astonish. His modest "wonders", which he designs by the imaginative intellect and builds by his free will, are metaphors of miracles, since man is a limping metaphor of God. Man is in God's "image" by having a creative intellect, active imagination and free will. "In him we live and move and have our being" (Acts 17:28). This was an ancient intuition, however inchoate, and St. Paul harked back six centuries to the diction of the poet Epimenides to remind the Greeks of it. Depression and sin reduce the ability to use these gifts proper to the divine image properly; still they are there. Man-made wonders are instinctive tributes to the splendor of God who willed man into being. Milk suffices for the infant, but as we grow we look for ice cream. The wheel is crafted in the first phase of technology, but invention spins it into a carousel. Words develop anthropologically, but there is a moment when they shape into song. As long as we are alive, we want to make life lively, and each fantastic effort is homage to the source of being. "We know that the whole creation has been groaning in travail together until now; and not only the whole creation, but we ourselves who have the first fruits of the Spirit groan inwardly as we wait for adoption as sons, the redemption of our bodies" (Rom 8:22–23).

Groan enough and marvelous things take shape: temples and towers, prodigies for every taste and passion. Not each builder of such wonders had an ecclesiastical tinge or necessarily thought lofty ideals in building lofty structures. That really does not matter. "Thoughts beyond their thoughts to those high bards were given" (John Keble). And when the builders die, or when their voices and imaginings run to lesser matters, the buildings keep witness to that fine description of wonder as involuntary praise. "God is able from these stones to raise up children to Abraham" (Mt 3:9). And when the God-Man who said that stood at the gates of Jerusalem, he raised it to a shout: "I tell you, if these were silent, the very stones would cry out" (Lk 19:40). When he performed the greatest of all the world's wonders in the Resurrection, he announced it with the solemn rolling away of a great stone.

Traditional canons counted stones and generally came up with what they called the Seven Wonders of the Ancient World. The typical list was defined by Antipater of Sidon in the second century before Christ; and Pliny the Elder was writing about some of them in a touristy way as the apostles were well out on their journeys. For our purposes these Seven Wonders take on a significance apart from any intention of their builders. Each of them is a point of reference for the Seven Words from the Cross with which our Lord defined the purpose of man in history. Attempted parallels can be as artificial as anything else contrived by a fabricator's imagination. But the definitive wonder is that two pieces of wood from which Christ spoke surpass in importance anything else carved and joined; and his few words ring louder to time's end than all the hearty and heartbreaking declamations of fine engineers and sculptors on the scaffolds of alabaster parapets.

I

THE STATUE OF ZEUS

"Father, forgive them, for they know not what they do."

Zeus on High

Among the seven ancient wonders, the statue of Zeus at Olympia in the Peloponnesus of Greece, looming over the Aegean between Thessaly and Macedonia, had preeminence if only because Zeus ranked first in the pagan pantheon. As far as size goes, at about forty feet, maybe sixty counting the base, this certainly was not the largest of the wonders, though its scale was remarkable enough and was meant to be so. If the proportions do not particularly impress the contemporary eye, we are not cleverer, we have just been at this sort of thing longer.

Each of the ancient accomplishments paraded technical skill as proof of the intellect and size as an extravaganza of the human will. The soul is the composite of intellect and will, and so the marvels of human hands are the soul's boasts, even when they are the work of those for whom a soul may be more enigmatic than mysterious. But to the point, things big are not necessarily things great; the statue on Olympus would not have been so wonderful were it not so beautiful. This was a god and not a giant: Zeus had a beauty Behemoth lacked. In the modern world, Americans have tended to measure a building by its cost, the English by its age and the Russians by its size. In the ancient world, wonders were made of all three, but all of these would have been irrelevant had they not been beautiful. Beauty, after all, is in the line of truth, and so it has to do with proportion rather than size.

When the first humans wanted to be like God, they did not try to grow larger; they went after the secret of proportions. The knowledge of good and evil they sought was the ability to define symmetry. The Fall of Man did not come because man realistically wanted information; it was the result of unrealistically wanting to be the Informer. It began the cult of self-expression, which fouled modern art. This was not the classical canon of beauty. Beauty expresses truth and can only express the self when the self is true. Otherwise we say seriously what Lewis Carroll said satirically in *The Hunting of the Snark*: "What I tell you three times is true." That is quite the opposite of the holy angels who say "Holy" three times because they are astonished that truth is true.

The Greeks had the idea of symmetry, if they did not have the revelation of perfect beauty. And to express it, they set out to impress themselves with it. The statue of Zeus was a prodigy of proportion, designed around 457 B.C. by Phidias, whom Western critics with only slight insularity call the father of sculpture. The great god's flesh was of ivory, in robes and ornaments of solid gold; so Phidias called the style "chryselephantine", of which there was a slight revival in the *art moderne* figurines of look-alike Isadora Duncan dancing ladies, with brass instead of gold. Zeus had precious stones to make the irises of his eyes flash, and he was seated to command mere mortals, who stood before him as trespassing artifacts in his fearsome temple. Zeus, strained through the sieves of myth, was the son of Saturn and brother to Neptune, the god of the sea, and Pluto, the god of the underworld. He survived when Saturn devoured his other children, and he eventually became King of the Heavens by deposing his father.

That is the kind of god we make when we craft gods. The symmetry that tempered the gigantism of their flesh had no sway over the extravagance of their morals. "You Greeks", said Justin Martyr in the *Discourse to the Greeks*, "should read aloud to Jupiter (Zeus) the law against parricide, the punishment for adultery and the stigma of pederasty." Zeus was so plausible in terms of human proclivities, virtues and vices writ large, that eventually even the keepers of his sanctuary knew him to be an invention; Suetonius says that Tiberius, who was emperor at the time of the Crucifixion, began consulting the stars instead of Jupiter-Zeus. The modern atheists have been like that, claiming the death of God and turning instead to fatalism, sometimes in the form of horoscopes and sometimes in the form of economic systems. God is made an inside joke, while superstitions are approached more gravely than the grave itself.

Beauty and Nature

When the civilized lose faith in beautiful gods, they make a god of beauty. That certainly was the case with late imperial Rome, it marked the lesser aesthetic movements of the Renaissance and late Victorian age, and in our generation it has virtually made art museums into shrines while turning many shrines into art museums. The Louvre becomes the Lourdes of the *cognoscenti*. Ultimately, the Catholic sacramental view is the unique safeguard against pagan aestheticism; not because of the way it invalidates paganism but precisely because of the way it validates the integration of beauty and virtue that chime-charmed paganism sensed but did not know.

The Catholic spirit values the pagan mind at least in its intuition of the beautiful. Puritanism, on the other hand,

considers all art an intrusion to nature. Puritan Christianity
is a contradiction in terms, though there are Puritan Christians, and in aesthetical terms the Catholic and the pagan
have more in common than either has with them. St. Paul
grounded his appeal on Mars Hill in this sensibility: "Men of
Athens, I perceive that in every way you are very religious"
(Acts 17:22). But as an apostle of the true revelation, his
preaching went beyond renaming one of their named gods;
he declared the Name of their one Unknown God. "The
first wonder is the offering of ignorance," said Coleridge,
"the last is the parent of adoration."

Through the rocks of Olympus and the roods of Char-
tres, beauty speaks as the voice of nature and uses the language of art; in the reduced Christian vision of the Puritan,
art is artifice stuck on nature like a patch to hide a blemish.
For the Puritan, beauty is either frivolity or mummery, and
there is no artist who is not a dilettante dabbling where
Adam fell. Sacred images would be subpoenaed in cathe-
drals, indicted for exposing themselves and locked up in gal-
leries. There the neo-pagans arrive to "make sense" of what
they see. But they cannot, because they are as suspicious of
nature as was the Puritan. There is little basic difference;
where the Puritan thought no one should delight in art, the
neo-pagan thinks only he should delight in it. Neither
understands that all art is for God's delight and that man
finds pleasure in it because he is in God's image. Puritanism
supposes that because there are vain pomps of the world, all
the world's pomps are vain, and ritual celebrations are inevitably frivolous, like children dressing up in their parents'
clothes to play house. Revived paganism dresses celebration
in nothing but our own small clothes and calls it with
affected dignity a "celebration of life". And because it lacks
Catholic balance, the pagan revival cannot escape a puritanical guilt at the same time: its own celebrations are wrapped

in the damp garments of didactic and relentlessly edifying commentary.

It should not surprise, then, to find that the new pagans, or "Modernists", have sought to dismantle churches just as the old puritans, or "Jansenists", did, smashing statues and covering marbles. In solemn worship of the self, they reduce ritual paraphernalia to microphones amplifying the self's voice, and the texts become slogans advertising the benefits of kindness, self-esteem and nice weather. David's dance before the ark becomes a pious form of recreational therapy. Puritan and pagan share a common hostility to temples because Puritan and pagan are ever fraught with fear. They are so bound up in themselves that the rumor of an unbound Sacred One who for their sake took on boundaries, and even willed to be bound against a Cross, haunts like a specter. In that psychology, a Holy House is a Haunted House. The puritanical solution is to turn it into a Meeting House. The pagan alternative is to make it a Fun House.

On Imagination and Wishful Thinking

By divine revelation, Moses got the objective reality of God right long before Socrates got it right by half. Origen had to make clear in the third century that "Moses and the prophets . . . are earlier not only than Plato but also than Homer and the discovery of writing among the Greeks." Whatever the human imagination invents apart from divine revelation is plausible to that imagination, and so it is inherently absurd when it claims to be beyond the human imagination, as when the pagan idols were supposed to be wiser than their sculptors and were said to inhabit heavens more cavernous than their temples. The reasonableness of gods made in the image of man is a reverse indicator of the truth of the un-imaginable, yet not irrational, depth of the Holy Trinity. The gods of the Greek and Roman pagans were larger than life; they were superhuman in contradistinction to the Three Persons of the Holy Trinity, who have no magnitude and who are deeper than life as human reason knows it, or, as we say, supernatural.

Oriental paganism takes another route, erring in the way of exoticism, where Occidental paganism went for natural-ism. As in the West divinity was larger than life even when it conformed to the canons of proportion, in the East divinity was more complicated than life: Zeus has two mighty biceps, Vishnu has four willowy limbs. So long as the pagans did not reconcile man and eternity, they oscillated between idols titanic or spidery. But the Holy Trinity has no size at all and is unspeakable simplicity rather than complication. When the Second Person incarnates, he is not gigantic, and he speaks in parables instead of conundrums. His Father's house has many rooms, but it is not a maze. The pagan idiom is perennial in its unaided imagination, and thus the sham paganism of a modern prejudice assumed that any concept of divinity must be voluntarist human projection. To the contrary, Christ is a divine injection, the sacrament of his Father, unexpected even by those who had been told prophetically to expect him. "Have I been with you so long, and yet you do not know me, Philip? He who has seen me has seen the Father; how can you say, 'Show us the Father'?" (Jn 14:9).

The mythical gods were amplifications of the human con-dition, so it took noise to get their attention. Their clients clapped hands for a hearing, as they still do in some oriental religions on entering a temple. And as the gods were proud, they were susceptible to flattery. We are dealing with gods not remote, just hard to get. Monsignor Knox told how worshippers would call to them the way fishermen cast flies, hoping one would lure a bite with lines like: "*Matutine pater, seu Jane libentius audis.*" "Father of the morning, or Janus if you'd rather hear it that way." On the Cross, Christ calls out in a wildly different way. As an anvil of flesh under the hammers, he comes close to spilling out unbearable secrets of the trinitarian economy, and among them is the absolute confidence the Son has of the Father's being and power. In the first of his words, Christ cries, "Father, forgive them for they know not what they do." Being and doing are one and the same for God, but the human struggle is to reconcile the two: imperfect actions contradict being. The crucifiers do not know what they are doing because they do not know who they are. They certainly do not know that they are brothers and sisters of the same man on the Cross, who is also the Son of God and their true God himself.

The Fathering God

The Passion is the glorification of the Son by the Father (Jn 12:23, 27–28; 17:1) and the passing of the Son to the Father (Jn 13:1). This we have from Christ himself. If society plunges into a frigid new paganism, it slips away from Christ's exposition of the Divine Fatherhood. Freud led the intellectual pack in confusing the idea of God with the search for a father image; but the authority on Christian existentialism, Professor John Macquarrie, says plainly in his *Twentieth Century Religious Thought*, "The question as to whether this analogue (God the Father) stands for any reality, or, if it does so, worthily represents it, is one on which psychoanalysis sheds no light whatever. . . . Jung is of course quite clear that the objective validity of religious beliefs is not a question for psychology." And we might say the same thing about religion questioned by anthropology when the Fatherhood of God is attributed to cultural patriarchy. The idea of a Father God is not a self-projection, because fatherhood is not an intuitive concept as is motherhood. Mothers know by nature how to mother; fathers are taught by mothers, and by the enforced disciplines of culture, how to father.

When a society begins to fall apart, first the fathers disappear. It has always been easy to speak of the closest things, what are called "nature", as maternal. The first word to form from the infant usually means Mother. It takes a tutored perception to speak of Father. We naturally conceive of what can conceive us; we have to be shown what can perceive us. Deny that naturalness and you also deny the supernaturalness revealed through it, and then unnaturalness in various forms takes its place. First appears the cult of science, in which technology poses as pompous theology, as at the rise of Modernism; and then the cult of the self, in which psychology speaks as nervous theology, as in the noon of Modernism; and now with the cult of nature, in which ecology acts as savage theology, in the twilight of Modernism.

A plain refutation answers those who say the Fatherhood of God is a projection of human patriarchy: Human patriarchy is at best a derivative symbol of the Fatherhood of God. To speak of fathers of families and fathers of nations and even calling the sculptor of Zeus's statue the father of sculpture are grammatical devices to express the power to start life. That power is not created as by an engine but is received as an endowment by the one Life-Giver. "For this reason I bow my knees before the Father, from whom every family in heaven and on earth is named . . ." (Eph 3:14). Against the backdrop of all that our Lord did among us, this cannot mean in an unimaginatively anthropomorphic way that divinity is male and not female; it does mean that analogically divinity is to nature fatherly rather than motherly, perceiving through eternity what nature will conceive. The God of Abraham and of Isaac and of Jacob is so strong he is positively paternal; he is too strong to be merely paternalistic.

Now, Aristotle mistook female receptivity for inert passivity, and Aquinas repeated the confusion in his biologism. Receptivity is a kinetic and vital attribute. Nature gives "delight" to God by receiving the gift of existence; Mary's "passivity" at the foot of the Cross represents the activity of the faithful human remnant, standing instead of prone, actively receiving a sword in her own heart. And so, too, our Holy Mother the Church is aroused to mission when she receives the Holy Spirit after days of waiting. There are those, it is true, who call these terms mere role-playing. What of that? The roles belong to the divine drama, and playing is not unreal when this is the world's one real play. Without the slightest defamation of the holy equality between the sexes, and indeed in its substantial support, matriarchy may in intuitive opinion be more godly; patriarchy is in revealed fact more godlike.

Carried to a more precise distinction with patriarchy, the fatherliness of God is analogous, while the Fatherhood of God is exact. Christ never spoke of his heavenly Father as though he were using a figure of speech. He used a kaleidoscope of images and a calliope of sounds to speak about God and eternity (shepherds, kings, pearls, mustard and weddings), but when he spoke to God, he said Father. And when he would be clearer, he used the intimate "Abba". He became most specific when he rose from the dead, confounding those who to this day would pretend the Resurrection was an abstraction. From Easter Day, he puts aside parables and puzzles and gives clear instructions. Having taught as it were by paintings on glass, he opens those windows for the forty days of Easter and shows the light that had been known remotely as illumination. And what does he choose to say to Mary Magdalen on the first Easter morning in this plain speech shorn of analogy? "Go to my brethren and tell them: I ascend to my Father and your Father, to my God and your God" (Jn 20:17). From then on, as the Gnostics at least have to admit, if you want to ignore the Fatherhood of God, you have to ignore the Resurrection and all that the risen Christ said and did.

If the Fatherhood of God were clearer than that, it would not be visible at all. Its eternal force is usually exposed by its obscurity in time and space. If the human eye sees through a glass darkly now, at least it sees an honest reflection and not a self-projection. We know what we are, but it is painfully unclear what we shall be. From the Cross, Christ's grand voice starts to sound like breaking glass, crying to the Father to forgive those who are smashing him. The noblest pagan would not cry out that way, let alone imagine a god doing it. While the gods helped the good and ignored the sufferings of the evil, "Christ gave assistance in equal measure to the good and the evil." So wrote Arnobius in the fourth century, and, as post-modern people flirt with new paganisms, they may find that just as problematic at the end of the twentieth century. But the imagination is one thing, the true image another: "Do not lie to one another, seeing that you have put off the old nature with its practices and have put on the new nature, which is being renewed in knowledge after the image of its creator" (Col 3:10).

Christ Lifted Up

Idols have height; Christ has stature. He looms over the ages, as the frozen decorum of an idol does not, nor is he brooding like a hapless clergyman seated on an elevated presidential chair where once stood the Tabernacle of the Blessed Sacrament. "Now is the judgment of this world, now shall the ruler of this world be cast out; and I when I am lifted up from the earth, will draw all men to myself" (Jn 12:31–32). The term "lifted up" can, and indeed does, mean to ascend to a cross and to the heavens. There is no incongruity in Christ's appearance being so different from the idols: instead of ivory flesh, he is torn and red, crowned with thorns, not gold, with possibly a hard saddle for a throne, because in the crucifixion system a little support like that raised the rib cage and prolonged the suffering of asphyxiation. Zeus had rubies and diamonds for eyes; Christ's are all bloodshot. And for a wand, Zeus held one of gold in his cold hand; Christ holds nothing. Napoleon told his soldiers that each of them carried in his cartridge pouch the baton of a marshal of France; and between 1804 and 1814, he made 26 marshals, besides 924 generals, but he made not one saint. Christ promises nothing but crosses; he was attached to nothing in this world but a cross himself.

Each cross received in this life is a chance to be raised up with Christ; each crucifixion can be a canonization, and each sickness and financial crisis and humiliation and betrayal can be a clandestine coronation. Because Christ suffered, we can be like him by suffering, if the suffering is received with thanks as a gift in defiance of the temptation to be saddened by it as by a curse. The mysterious concept of holy mortification in healthy Christian tradition stems from this; and St. Gregory the Great virtually hymned to it when he said that they who would be humble without being despised, or happy with one's lot without being needy, or chaste without mortifying the body, are like soldiers who flee the battlefield and try to win the war from within the city's walls. On Good Friday a whole mob like that fled Calvary for the city enclosure. The moral fact of this fleshes out all anthropology: there are two kinds of people. There are those who worship Christ, and they are crucified with him; and there are those who worship themselves, and they crucify him.

Idols have been enthroned, enshrined and carried about on gaudy pallets; they have never been crucified, if only because they would break. There were the gods of Epicurus, who "live where there is no rain or snow, where never tempest blows". In pagan legends the idolized gods came down verdant hills to mingle however disdainfully with more fragile mortals. Christ dragged his Cross up a hill. Calvary has been a greater wonder since then than Mount Olympus, and the Lord of Calvary vastly more challenging to the human imagination than the Lord of Olympus. As for his divinity, it was suppressed in his human appearing by willed humility, so that when it shone it was as a fleeting spark from a covered fire; his mortal years were the curfew of heaven, and never more so than when the sky itself pulled its shades on Good Friday. His humanity was serene by a design that made the Greek golden mean practically unbalanced by comparison; he wove his way through the world sternly without cruelty, gently without sentimentality, vernacularly without vulgarity, mysteriously without obscurity—he hid when the crowds tried to publicize him, and when he hung exposed the crowds crept away as from an awful secret. This is not the life of idols, but it is the way of Life himself.

Here is the answer to why, ever since, anything crucial has had to do with the Cross. In the Passion of Christ the seal was set on moral authenticity. Sins are a lot of things, but sin itself is escapism, because it would locate satisfaction in a massive insufficiency of living. And human virtues fill many lists, but virtue itself is the soul's hospitality to the source of reality, the Holy Trinity dwelling in the human deed. A saint is human, and specifically saints are the only humans, in contrast to sinners who claim to be only human; until man is a saint, he is less than a man and an exile from his human potential. The saint drives a car and programs computers and buys groceries like anyone else, but all the while the will of God is the saint's will in all his choices as he drives and programs and shops.

By detaching the human being from any definition of being less than human, holiness is the one artful and authentic way to be human. Detachment is a moral crucifixion, as it nails down those impulses and habits that lead the intellect to lie and the imagination to violate and the will to will its own way. Through the indwelling of the Holy Trinity, that is, through sanctifying grace, the intellect abjures lies and stands defiantly before armies of bullies and alliances of compromised parliaments; and the graced imagination laughs at fantasies when they come as painted hags or tinsel utopias or the penultimate chapter of a volume on how to be happy by feeling happy.

This reality is expensive, and sin is the method of avoiding such expense. The bargain basement turns out to be much lower than one could possibly have known or imagined or wanted. That is why it is so difficult to believe in hell. It is not beyond belief—it is wondrously beneath belief, and it takes humility to fathom a justice deeper than our altruistic sense of justice. The most melancholy moment in that infernal place may well be when words reach it faintly from the apostle whose preaching has no power there: "Do you not know that your body is a temple of the Holy Spirit within you, which you have from God? You are not your own; you were bought with a price. So glorify God in your body" (1 Cor 6:19–20).

The Most Divine Comedy

When the classical world lost faith in its gods, the life of its theatre dried up. It was hard to take drama on the stage seriously when the drama had evaporated from life itself. There were plays. But great plays about living, like those of Aristophanes, had become little plays on living, like those of Plautus, little more than elegantly worded sarcasms. Degeneracy set in as it always does when gods are found to be idols. Degeneration is generation without a will, a sort of grinding of gears pretending to move. It is what happens when a providential plan for life appears to be a cruel hoax of repetitiousness.

The Romans were not aware of the change, not suddenly anyway. When their gods died, their clients kept their festivals for a while, the way some moderns who have lost their Christianity without realizing it try to turn their religion into a folk phenomenon. There is, for instance, a folk form of "Cute Catholicism" built around ethnic food fairs and parades. The more nervous it grows about the claims of Christ on the soul, the more it diverts itself with self-conscious amiability; and the more it shrinks from challenging souls with the call to holiness, the more it assures sociologists of its harmlessness. Its priests may fill the gap in their lives by giving each other Man-of-the-Year awards and its nuns may dress as clowns to entertain bewildered children who have learning disabilities. There is a deep death rattle in all the hearty *bonhomie* and self-conscious chuckling. When gods go, their clients still climb on their carousels for festival and soon complain that they are just going in circles.

Unlike the Catholic with a zeal for souls, the Cute Catholic, for whom religion is a sentimental custom, feels guilty about Gospel evangelism and justifies his neglect of it by saying it is cultural imperialism; and unlike the convert, who is a curiosity and a threat to him, the Cute Catholic can never be certain whether he would be a Catholic if he had not been "born" one. When culture transforms faith, opposite the apostolic model, the Cute Catholic tries to establish his place in secular society by socializing his own faith. This he rationalizes as "the Church speaking to culture in modern terms", when of course it is culture dictating to the Church. If the Church makes her method an object of faith, she loses her faith: that is, if the definitive function of the Church is to fit human expectations, she quickly becomes disposable. The Cute Catholic will claim that he is speaking prophetically to his mauve decade when he attends Mass in golf clothing, in a Church made to look like his living room with wall-to-wall carpeting and potted plants, without a visible confessional, satisfied that there is no more stigma attached to being Catholic. And of course there can be no stigma attached, because stigmata are got from crosses, and when the Cute Catholic renovated his church, he removed the crucifix.

Denial of false gods historically has marked some new discovery about the self and the world, as when Akhenaton moved the Egyptian cult from polytheism to single worship of the Sun. Denial of the true God, conversely, is inevitably marked by a loss of self-identity and a fragmentation of cultural reference, most conspicuously in family life, legal theory and the philosophy of education. The divine comedy of living becomes tragic indeed, and never more pathetic than in the erosion of the sacred place and the sacred ritual of that place. And when the place held sacred is sacred to the truly holy, its desolation is wide and vast as the cosmos. As St. Thomas says in comparing moral disorder with physical cataclysms, "The goodness of grace in one single person is greater than the material good of the entire universe"

(S. Th. I-II, q. 113 a.). The statue of Zeus was destroyed by fire in A.D. 476, melting in a magnificently heart-rending pile of gold and broken jewels. The destruction of a Christian shrine may be sad from a nostalgic and aesthetic point of view, but for the virtuous it is a cleft in the very heart of the world.

When God Forgives

From just a scientifically critical point of view, the book of *The Acts of the Apostles* is an important stage in the development of historical narrative. The unadorned innocence of its domestic details in narrating such breathtaking events is a combination of Grandma Moses and Rembrandt. To read it is to come face to face with the totally unselfconscious yet startling change in the apostles' personalities after the Passion, Resurrection and gift of the Holy Spirit at Pentecost. They had been consistently straightforward and blunt men—no dual personalities; their change was radical, not the development of one trait over another. They had been petrified at the prospect of the Cross, and days later they seemed almost deified. In Lystra, the people rallied all their hyperbole to hail Barnabas as Zeus, and they called the diminutive Paul by the lesser name of the messenger of the gods, Hermes. It was a raucous scene, and especially so when a priest of Zeus led out oxen as a sacrifice along with floral offerings. As the priests of Jerusalem had torn their robes in horror at what they considered Christ's blasphemy in calling himself God, Barnabas and Paul tore their garments in the ritual Jewish way in horror, too, this time because they and not Christ were being accorded divinity. "Men, why are you doing this? We also are men, of like nature with you . . ." (Acts 14:15).

This had already happened to Peter of all people, problematic and once fallible Peter. After he had fallen asleep during our Lord's agony, he awoke to a voice calling him "Simon". It was a subtle reminder that he was slipping back to the old man: this was the only time Christ called him by his former name after he had changed it to Peter, which means Rock. Christ was trying to coax Peter's soul to birth at the moment it was withdrawing to the foetal position of all souls unresponsive to the new creature Christ offers to make of us. But Christ won out, and when Peter sees Cornelius kneeling before him in Caesarea, he cries out like Paul and Barnabas. The words are among the most frightening declarations in the human record, absurd if you think Christ made no difference in those days and annoying if you wish he had made none: "Stand up; I too am a man" (Acts 10:26).

The change was the work of grace upon personality, just as psychological disintegration is the work of sin. Personality is a metaphysical, or deeper than physical, quality of the physical person. Unless it responds to supernatural promptings, it calcifies into a caricature of its true potential. Jargonish phrases about human fulfillment and self-realization are untutored ways of grasping for this truth. Possibly with a sense of inevitable resignation, Einstein told his friend Carnap that the sense of the continuity of personal identity within a consciousness of the present is outside the realm of physics. Holiness as the perfection of personality based on a consciousness of eternity cannot be less so.

Unaided psychology does not explain the change that happened to Christ's followers. Natural science, when true to itself, can acknowledge the existence of saints as facts, but it cannot account for the sanctity itself. As Newman said of physics applied to any problem, "With matter it begins, with matter it will end." The unscientific reaction to the obvious transformation of such men as Peter is to drop the subject. It is really quite amazing how widespread this tendency is. You would expect that psychologists would be fascinated with saints; but in psychological studies saints figure, if at all, as hysterics or zealots. The changed lives of saints have changed history more than any other phenomenon, and they are not mentioned in most university history texts. This avoidance is a form of cultural pathology, a contemporary repetition of the way the Sanhedrin covered their ears when the Redeemer spoke. And that denial is itself mute testimony to the greatest wonder in the world.

Idols cannot disturb the human conscience that way. They cannot threaten self-proclaimed realists to the point of denying reality. They embody the denial in themselves. By enlarging life, they are boundaries beyond which life cannot change. If you bow before an idol, it will not say, "Stand up; I too am a man." That is the one thing an idolater will not tolerate. He has made his gods, and he will have them act as gods as he has made gods to be. They are fantasy, and to the realist there is nothing more plausible than a fantasy he has built himself. When an idol falls, as the Zeus of Phidias collapsed in flames, the mind can make a mental image of its ghost, and nothing is lost, because there was no substance behind the form to begin with. A god in the image of a man is in the image of a man's imagination. This knowledge, which was vouchsafed to the Jews, fascinated the cautious Romans. In the first century, the writer Silius Italicus was intrigued by the way Hannibal, evidently influenced by his Semitic roots, had prayed some three centuries earlier in a temple in what is now Cadiz to a god who had no physical depiction. The absence of a statue of a god was almost as astonishing as the appearing of a god might have been.

The Psalmist was so inspired that he stated the obvious about idols: they have mouths that do not speak. Christ did speak. He used acoustical effects to be heard, like speaking from mountain tops, and from a boat so that the water of Galilee would be an amplifier. The Cross was a sounding board when he was locked against it. Should Zeus and his family of lesser gamboling gods move their marble lips, they might rain down fiery vengeance or glittery bromides. One sentence they would not speak. From the time it sounded from the Cross, it has changed men and women of ill disposition and weak will into human humans: "Father, forgive them, for they know not what they do."

II

THE PYRAMIDS OF EGYPT

"Truly, I say to you, today you will be with me in Paradise."

The One Surviving Wonder

By any measure and from any distance, the Cross was a splinter on the skin of the earth, surely irrelevant next to any monument. As Christ hung on it ignominiously, the tallest construction known to the classical diarists was the Great Pyramid of Khufu, or Cheops to the Greeks, which at 481 feet held the record for some 4500 years. This and the other massive pyramids of Khafra and Menkaura, built between 3000 and 1800 B.C. in Giza, or Al Jizah, laid indubitable claim to rank among the wonders of the world, and the Great Pyramid still is the largest stone building in existence. The tomb of the Pharaoh Khufu was built late in the twenty-sixth century before the Incarnation; by the time of Christ's appearance on earth, it had become a symbol of massive antiquity to people we think of as antique.

Given their size, the one unsurprising fact about pyramids is that they remain, the only extant wonder of the classical seven. Khufu had two million three hundred thousand blocks of limestone, and some of granite, averaging two and a half tons each, and a few weighing thirty tons. Its polished surfaces glared in the sun like nearly perfect mirrors. One hundred thousand workers labored on it for twenty years, from its foundation, covering more than thirteen acres, to the fine point of its pinnacle. This was not always cruelly done, contrary to received opinion and more than a few overwrought films. Herodotus fell for fantastic reports of

100,000 slaves working on the Great Pyramid. Slaves slaved, it is true, and burnt men ate dry crusts; but principally in the appalling copper and gold mines of the Sudan, Sinai and Nubia. Slavery was most widespread only with the New Kingdom beginning with the Eighteenth Dynasty in 1567 B.C.; by the Twentieth Dynasty, Rameses III could deploy 130,000 slaves on his temple project. Work on the pyramids was a different case. Most of the laborers were free citizens whose rights generally were respected; the world's first strike took place around 1170 B.C., when craftsmen at the Necropolis in Thebes demanded, and received, a couple of months' back pay. The royal tombs provided a form of work relief program for the people who were without work when the Nile flooded its banks late in the summer. Even without that incentive, many would have volunteered to be involved in a mystical project with so many promised rewards in the next life. A contemporary record says that there often was a celebratory air and the men "came home in good spirits, sated with bread, drunk with beer, as if it were the beautiful festival of a god".

In 1922 the expedition of Lord Carnarvon unlocked the secret of one of the buried tombs in the Valley of the Kings, that of a relatively unimportant son-in-law of Queen Nefertiti. When the chamber was opened, the Earl's colleague, Howard Carter, stood frozen by the splendor reflected in the timid light of his candle, the unleashed air rushing at him with wild whispers thousands of years in waiting: "strange animals, statues and gold—everywhere the glint of gold". When the 242-pound solid gold inner coffin of the Pharaoh Tutankhamen was opened and the aureole mask, aching in beauty, lifted, the head was found crowned with floral wreaths still identifiable, dried by nearly thirty-three hundred years: careful hands had woven for him a frail coronet of cornflowers and blossoms of the mandrake, the symbol of love and immortality mentioned in Genesis and the Song of Solomon. The face was discernible, though an embalming unguent had dyed it a deep black. Carter could not forget his first glimpse: "A serene and placid countenance, that of a young man." This same desiccated visage with vacant eyes had been staring into the dark that way when the child Jesus was brought exiled into Egypt's searing light of day, as fresh-faced as the ancient-young pharaoh was drawn and leathered like all the other mummified kings. And it lay there in the same position, not a fraction moved, when the man Jesus hung nailed to the Cross with living eyes toiling under the sun.

The Pharaoh and the Messiah

A truth so vast and inclusive as the universal redemptive power of Christ, a fact so uncompromising in its absolute claim to revelation as the Christian promise of eternal life, an historical interpretation so confident as that of the Christian Church, will have to be true in its claims or totally false. As they are human inventions, philosophies and economies and mythologies are not like that. They can be modified to refine partial truths from their fallible analyses. Even heresies have some orthodox point within their erroneous constitutions, from which they become deviant. They begin with a right premise; they make it the only right premise.

But Christianity is wholly different. It is as whole as it is true. Everything about it is the heart of the matter. To take out any part of it is to take the heart out of it, and to take the heart out of it is to take out all of it. "Think not that I have come to abolish the law and the prophets; I have come not to abolish them but to fulfill them. For truly, I say to you, till heaven and earth pass away, not an iota, not a dot, will pass from the law until all is accomplished" (Mt 5:18). This is the moral geography then in which the little splinter of the Cross set up on Golgotha is the core of the universe and the pyramids are pebbles shying in its shadow. The face grimacing on the Cross gives a clue to why other faces in every age and place before and since Good Friday have been garlanded in death more reverently than in life. If the eyes of the pharaohs had often in life searched caves and skies for some space to live after death, they did so because the truth of Christ is eternal. It should not seem odd to find this same truth stammered through myriad intuitions before Christ is born and after he dies. "The wind blows where it wills, and you hear the sound of it, but you do not know whence it comes or whither it goes . . ." (Jn 3:8).

A partial truth is by its partiality a thing different, and sometimes disquietingly different, from the complete truth of the Holy Spirit. But even degeneration can bear negative testimony to the need for regeneration. Each time an Aztec priest put on parrot plumes to cut out a human heart, the rampant drums beat an ignorant upside-down hymn to the great High Priest whose own heart was pierced on a Cross as a sacrifice for his people. By special selection the ups and downs of the Hebrew tribes were meant to fulfill an obscure but certain plan of which they were part. "And as Moses lifted up the serpent in the wilderness, so must the Son of Man be lifted up that whoever believes in him may have eternal life" (Jn 3:14–15).

The Jews themselves were not of one mind on the subject of life after death, and this became notorious after the actual Resurrection. With inspired shrewdness, the apostle Paul ingratiated himself with the Pharisees against the Sadducees, who would chase the articulated concept of a resurrection out of court. The violence with which they debated was its own evidence for the tenuousness of their case. The

Sadducean party was modern in its contempt for super-natural facts. Flavius Josephus recorded how not only did the Sadducees believe the soul dies with the body and observe nothing more than what the Law enjoined them, "they think it an instance of virtue to dispute with those doctors of philosophy whom they frequent. Their doctrine is received but by a few, yet by those of the greatest dignity." On the periphery of this chosen people every less disputatious intimation of immortality was a shy mutter of what would become the proclamation of resurrection. To Romans like the governor Festus, the proclamation was an absurdity added to the incongruity of Judaism. In one of literature's boldest throwaway lines, he mentioned to King Agrippa "one Jesus who was dead, but whom Paul asserted to be alive" (Acts 25:19). But even suave Romans were haunted by apparitions they knew could not exist.

To trace these concerns outside Christian thought is not to go the way of the theologian who thought there could be "anonymous Christianity", as though all moral ideas boil up to the same revelation. But one might venture to discern the shape of anonymous Christians, if not Christianity, feeling their way to God by natural evidences, while not yet aware of the Holy Spirit who alone gives new life. There do seem to be long and longing shadows of hope cast by those who embalmed bodies in Egyptian deserts, or sank them in Scandinavian peat bogs. Something braver than resigned pathos made tribes weave flower crowns for ashen brows. Of course it is a kind of melancholy hope without the Christian realism that refuses to deny the fact of death. Paganism hopes against hope; the Church hopes. When you pitch the virtue of hope against itself, you end up with a vestigial Stoic stiff upper lip. When you look closely, it is trembling. In more modern times it became a pose known as the *élan vital*, the ineffable life force. Now this has come to mean many things, but it has consistently meant that if we see mortality through to its end, we will be through with it. Such persistence pretends to a vitality of its own that transcends death, as if you could overcome death by going over it. It is not much of a philosophy.

A stiff upper lip ensures nothing but speechlessness. It is not anything like the faintly amused lips on the Christian icons of Ravenna and Rome. Christianity does a thing more daring than hoping in spite of death, as though it might evaporate death; it positively spites death. The Cross was made important by the empty tomb, but it, and not the empty tomb, became the central Christian symbol to make this point. You cannot overcome death unless you go through it. The Lord promises that whoever lives and believes in him will never die, but that promise is made to him who believes "though he die" (Jn 11:25). Resurrection is realism compounded: it insists with a logic uncompromised by the sentimentality of sin that death like everything else must die.

Some Parallels

Cardinal Newman reminded a Vatican official that the people of Birmingham have souls, too; we have tried to remind ourselves that in ancient times people had souls. Though their times were ancient, their souls were no more "ancient" than ours are "up-to-date". A soul is eternity's disclosure of itself to the temporary condition of a person. The information and disinformation pondered by souls long ago made some sense of the truth about eternal life both by their affirmations and by their contradictions. According to the theory developed up to the New Kingdom, a pharaoh held the key to eternity by his influence with Osiris, the god of the afterlife. Dank though this cobwebbed world was, it hinted at the later promise: "So whoever acknowledges me before men, I also will acknowledge before my Father who is in heaven" (Mt 10:32; cf. Lk 12:8). The solemn pharaohs were supposed to have power to intercede with Anubis, god of embalming and protector of the dead, who led lesser mortals into the next world. But as they lay entombed in golden stillness, Jesus would stand with arms outstretched in a Jerusalem garden on the night of his betrayal: "Father, the hour has come; glorify thy Son that the Son may glorify thee, since thou hast given him power over all flesh, to give eternal life to all whom thou hast given to him" (Jn 17:1–2).

It was the practice for Egyptian courtiers to paint their names on walls close to Pharaoh's sarcophagus, as though they might live on if only by association. The custom was given vitality by the early Christians writing their names on the walls of the catacombs near the bones of apostles and martyrs, and for a more certain hope, of more than an after-life, of a new life in a new City open to "only those who are written in the Lamb's book of life" (Rev 21:27). At the completion of the Khufu pyramid, twelve villages were charged to keep vigil for Pharaoh's soul; Christ charged twelve men to pray for all souls. An entombed immortality had not a shred of the vitality promised by rebirth, and there is then a world of theology in the furtive way men brought to a cradle in Bethlehem the embalming ointment that the devotees of Egyptian cults brought to a tomb. And by another reverse, when sad hands had made a ritual of placing crowns of flowers on their king's head, the man who was labeled a king on the Cross was given a crown of thorns.

These may be too neat as parallels. One remains inescapable because history has engraved it in the very stone. It has to do with the tombs themselves. Edifying tracts have remarked countless times the most remarkable recollection in the memory of human events, an anecdote to defuse the entire repertoire of epics rhymed against the power of God, and it is this: the sarcophagus of Pharaoh kept the remains of Pharaoh within it, and the tomb of Christ was found empty only three days into the rest of history. Archeologists like Lord Carnarvon got their museums and the Lord of Creation got his Church.

The Use of Right Reason

None of what we have been discussing would have slightly interested the two men who were crucified with Jesus. The attention span of a man being crucified is limited. The rational powers are sorely tested and quickly wear if only by the physical facts. Unremitting pain, asphyxiation, delirium, exposure and dehydration are not the stuff of a seminar, not on any subject. All the more remarkable, then, are how the one man reasons and the reason he gives when the other mocked the Messiah: "Do you not fear God, since you are under the same sentence of condemnation? And we indeed justly; for we are receiving the due reward of our deeds; but this man has done nothing wrong" (Lk 23:41).

Nothing wrong! Here is the whole sum of human judgment, the nobility and frailty of every consultation and jury and parliament on record. It is the last desperate human judgment on the one who by any calculation, natural or inspired, was the most perfect human. Nothing wrong! If we understood the full weight of what that meant, no more books would be written, and nothing more would be said unless it were sung. This man has done nothing wrong.

Of course perfection did not become a man to make us do nothing wrong; he came to right wrong itself and to

make us right with him. In the same sense, sacramental confession wipes away sin but does not leave it at that; the slate
is erased to be written on, and the writer is the living Word
himself. Pharaoh could not write on the human heart, he
could not engrave true identities on souls; he did many
wrong things, and when he did, his people were only
obliged to say that it was right for him to do what was
wrong. The impeccability of Christ was a tangible power of
access to the unfamiliar dimension of eternity. Pontius Pilate
became so unnerved when he glanced into it that he called
out three times, "I find no crime in him" (Jn 18:38; 19:4;
19:6; cf. Lk 23:4, 14). By this faint exasperation, he tried to
pull himself out of the dizzying moral swirl, nostalgic for the
noble simplicity of the bucolic Roman virtues that no
longer lived even in Rome, certainly not in the marbleized
and renovated Rome where he had staked his career. Pilate
only said what the Good Thief would say; and had he only
been willing to follow through his line of reasoning, he too
might have been assured eternity. "To him who conquers I
will grant to eat of the tree of life, which is in the paradise of
God" (Rev 2:7).

Reasoning It Out

The Passion of Christ had a rational architecture of its own,
and the halting attempts of various characters to assess Christ
of the Passion at least were efforts at reason. Latin Pilate was
trying to be rational in a city for whose oriental irrationality
he could not conceal contempt. He flung the whole farce
into the hands of the venomous mob and scribbled one
audacious note of reason on a placard: "King of the Jews".

Our Creator has given us reason because he wants us to
use it. Christ is relentlessly and sublimely rational through-

out his agony, turning courtrooms into classrooms and teaching even as he collapses on the road to Calvary. He is the culmination of a history in which civilizations have used their limited reason to express truths greater than the reasons for those truths. If the Passion is the ultimate architecture, great pharaonic buildings are reason's own prophecy that God who made the world would one day rebuild it, even though the pagan mind was practically oblivious to the significance of history as a purposeful continuum. The pyramids were monuments to the reason no less than to immortality. It is really quite wonderful to see how their foundational points were ordered according to the four points of the compass; the greatest pyramid of all was so aligned that the maximum error in the configuration of its sides was one twelfth of one degree, and the northeast corner is just one half inch lower than the southeast corner. Etienne Gilson said, "It is necessary to know geometry in order to construct a façade that may be an act of love." And before him Leonardo himself, no authority to be gainsaid, was as clear: "Painting is not solely a matter of the heart. It is first and foremost a thing of the mind." But without the Judaeo-Christian revelation of historical purpose, upon which modern scientific development is founded, Egyptian engineering progressed little after the Old Kingdom.

Counterfeit piety commits a sinister betrayal by hinting that rationality is a pretension of an inherently deprived nature and that true religion is irrational. That was the melancholy assessment of Reformation divines, but over a thousand years earlier St. Basil wrote in his monastic rule: "The love of God is not founded on a discipline imposed on us from outside but is constitutively established in us as the capacity and necessity of our nature." God's truth taxes the human reason highly, but it is not at the expense of human reason. Anyone who has thought so has been a menace in the annals of religion and a neophyte in the laboratories of science. We can learn from the way one modern army classified recruits. Most desirable were the bright and energetic. Second in preference were the bright and lazy. The third rate were the stupid and lazy. The least desirable were the stupid and energetic. In the history of God's way with man, the stupid and energetic have never been the saints; but they have killed many of the saints, and they nimbly shouted empty thoughts at Divine Wisdom fastened with nails.

If the agent intellect aims at truth and if God is Truth, why then are not all reasonable people believers in God? Instances of sheer ignorance aside, the answer has to do with the soul, of which reason is part, but only part. The soul also consists of a will that aims at one's good as reason aims at truth. That which is good is true, but that which is only one's concept of the truth is guaranteed to be only one's concept of the good. While faith and reason can "never be opposed to one another", as the First Vatican Council reiterated, "the doctrine of faith that God has revealed has not been proposed, like a philosophical invention, to be perfected by human intelligence but has been delivered as a divine deposit to the Spouse of Christ to be faithfully kept and infallibly declared" (*Dei Filius*, chap. IV). Until the will chooses to let one's good be God, the reason is its own undoing. Reasoning then is left as rationalizing, and rationalizing is a delectation of the ego, even when it is as charming as Dean Swift's syllogism: he refused to preach about divine mysteries because mysteries cannot be explained, and preaching about what cannot be explained is a waste of time.

"The heart has its reasons which reason knows nothing of", but so does heartlessness. You only have to look at the judges before whom Christ passed: the High Priest and Herod and Pilate. Each broke laws to justify their version of the law. This was even worse than breaking laws to justify one's version of justice. The guilty verdict that the High Priest got from a hastily summoned rump of the Great Sanhedrin was illegal by its own terms because it was unanimous, and unanimity was assumed to indicate inadequate representation of the defense. After Pilate declared Jesus innocent, he denied his own jurisdiction. After Herod found Jesus innocent in an exercise of jurisdiction, he returned him to the jurisdiction of Pilate, who compounded the confusion by passing a second sentence of punishment, which Roman law forbade.

But the definitive tragedy of the irrational ego was that of one apostle. Peter said that "Judas turned aside to go to his own place" (Acts 1:25). It is the recipe of every crime past and future. When Chesterton defined the madman as the man who has lost everything but his reason, he was looking at the desolate field into which Judas plunged headlong along with everyone else who identifies the will exclusively with the self.

Reason refined by the selfless will is as stern as it is reliable, and so Chesterton also wrote in *The Father Brown Omnibus*: "Reason is always reasonable, even in the last limbo, in the lost borderland of things. I know that people charge the Church with lowering reason, but it is just the other way. Alone on earth, the Church affirms that God himself is bound by reason." God requires of himself then that he give human will full reign even when it inflates human reason; the Savior is bound by his own reason to let Judas go off quickly into the night to do what his occluded conscience must do, and by the same reason he weeps over Jerusalem and then lets Jerusalem bind him to the Cross. The city eventually fell as the result of various ways by which various characters had used their reason to rationalize lies as though they were true.

In modern experience, Communism institutionalized willfulness until it managed to rationalize the facts of history, in a way not altogether unlike the obtuseness of Christ's judges. The Poles used to say that under the Communists only the future is certain, the past is always changing. That was much the way Christ's accusers read their own law and prophets to him. Then came the Resurrection, of which the fallen Berlin Wall and rising democratic voices in our present time are but small aftershocks. And crowds from Prague to Addis Ababa smiling on toppled statues of Lenin are reflecting the afterglow of fire from heaven. When Jerusalem's judges and interpreters of events thought they had wiped away the enigmatic Christ with their scouring logic, he was seen walking in the red sunset with red wounds still fresh, explaining to pale men on a road why the Passion had to have happened this red way.

Survival Is Not Enough

Humility is a virtuous guarantee of reason's right use. Humility, after all, is honesty, and the truth attained by dishonesty would be a novelty indeed. The Curé d'Ars, for example, scaled extraordinary heights of logic literally by his virtuosity as a humble man: when a visitor called him an ass, he answered that if Samson was able to slay a thousand Philistines with the jawbone of an ass, think how much an entire ass might do. Without humility an adult will do childish things. He will blame his lapse from religion on a nun who hit him with a foot-rule in the fifth grade. Has he deserted his wife to marry a younger woman? He says it is because he long harbored doubts about the validity of the vows he made as an immature groom. Does he leave the Church to join a sect that does not have sacramental confession? He protests it is because of his diligent research into the inauthenticity of papal infallibility. Does he contracept life in his suburban villa? It must be to alleviate hunger in Bangladesh.

As humility deals in truths, pride deals in lies; and among the most dismal lies is the atheist's belief that there is nothing to believe in except existence and nothing to live for except survival. It is absurdity on the scale of believing that the purpose of breathing is to avoid breathlessness; at once it is obviously true and totally false. Truths have to be connected to other truths if they are not to become lies. Up is up, but if upness is everything, down is not down. Existence is the first fact of being; when it is the only fact of being it becomes the esoteric philosophical form of madness known as existentialism.

This takes the adventurous inquirer back to the pyramids, for the Egyptian neurosis was the notion of survival as all-important. It was like supposing that we have teeth in order to brush them. The languid immortality sealed in the pyramids was in no way a reverence for life; it was in every way a reverence for not dying. Pharaoh did not die in order to live; he just expected to keep living when he died. Embalming was essential to that kind of living. Pharaoh promised his people an afterlife. Christ promised an eternal life. An Egyptian inscription called the tomb an "eternal home". But in a lifetime of providing for particulars, from providing meals for thousands to providing arrangements for one last supper, Christ provided himself with no tomb and just made a passing reference to being buried "three days and three nights in the heart of the earth" (Mt 12:40). He made no burial arrangements. He only made dying arrangements. That whole life was an arrangement for dying. "Now is my soul troubled. And what shall I say? 'Father, save me from this hour'? No, for this purpose I have come to this hour" (Jn 12:27).

The burial was haphazard, and within days the burial cloths were found cast aside, the head bandage gracefully rolled up, God's most nonchalant sign of contempt for self-preservation. When the last hieroglyphic is deciphered and the final sentences on the pyramids are read, one sentence will not be found, though it is the reason we have reason. It was written only once anywhere, on the Cross and in blood: "For whoever would save his life will lose it; and whoever loses his life for my sake, he will save it" (Lk 9:24).

An Offering of the Will

Survival is passive like the climate; resurrection is active like today's weather. Pharaoh lay down; Christ got up. The desire to survive in spite of death is a failure of the will to spite death by being raised from it. Surely bureaucracy is the epitome of the loss of will. The less confidence an institution has in its purpose, the more it spends its energy to survive. A dying institution can give the appearance of vitality, though this is by desperation: a dying body pants as fast as a runner, and a sinking ship may turn on all its lights and blow its siren the loudest. In such an institution the only growth is in the size of its faculties of maintenance, certainly not in its faculties of propagation. Swelling bureaucracies do not kill an institution; they are the bloating of a corpse already dead. There really is nothing much to do with so useless a left-over. It is rather like the marvelously preserved three-thousand-year-old mummy of Rameses III: an Egyptian official did not quite know what to call it for tax purposes when it was being shipped to Cairo in 1881, so he labeled it dried fish.

The Church would never have survived had she been a preservation society, and Christ would have been long forgotten had he organized a committee to keep it going. He sent out apostles flushed through with the Holy Spirit to "guide you into all the truth" (Jn 16:13). If this has become a truism, it is because it is a truth often repeated; and if it sounds dull, that is the penalty for having forsaken life-giving tradition for supine self-maintenance. True traditionalism is the medium of change, as it protects those institutions and values by which the growth of a thing becomes a vital tradition instead of a pathological metastasis. Change has to be traditional to prevent it from becoming cancerous. A tradition then is more than a form of conservation. When the progressivist, or modern liberal, turns from religion as the authentic tradition, he tends to panic about decay and death and winds up making conservation of nature a religion of itself. As it contradicts the economy of life and death, its own language is contradictory. Its literary taste for nature even inflates a term that is harmless in itself, though heroically self-contradictory: "the conservation movement". When people lose faith in salvation won on a tree, some of them inevitably will make a religion of saving trees.

There is that problematic verse of Henry Lyte: "Change and decay in all around I see . . .", as though the two were the same. Change may indicate decay, but in the temporal order lack of change ensures decay. God who is the Life-Giver "changeth not"; man is obliged to change constantly as the Life-receiver. We may not like change, but that is because the human race's first experience of change was the loss of aureole Paradise. The condition of sin is man not fully alive; and any new situation is as suspect as it is disruptive. The baby cries when it leaves the womb, and the critic casts a cold eye on each invention and new arrival on the block. The reactionary misses the point of tradition as haplessly as the progressivist. He becomes like the boy who told his music teacher that he could not find Middle C after she moved the piano.

The sacred tradition is a message alive from a tomb; it is far from a mummy in the tomb. The whole Christian tradition, "salvation history", is a motion from a first event through events toward their purpose. It is Genesis to Revelation through the Crucifixion. "Ways" was the term Thomas Aquinas used for his proofs: "*viae*" instead of static diagrams or cases. And it is right for any scholar to ponder how the last action of that greatest teacher was to ride a donkey along a road, singing all the while about sight and touch and taste and eternal life. If this harmony of time and eternity were better recognized and lived, it would be harder to caricature tradition as the enemy of change.

Universities have failed in modern society because of their rebellion against the sacred tradition. They have become monumental pyramids, hospices for the embalmed remains of what once was learning, now sustained by growing numbers of administrators and shrinking numbers of teachers, surviving on grants and measuring their viability by their endowments, static as the latter-day Egyptians who had seen the Old Kingdom pass.

Theology is the unifying reference for the pursuit of truth in all the human sciences, and when a university becomes atheistic, it is as dysfunctional as a man who becomes inhumane. What is now called "politically correct" language on the campuses is inarticulateness caused by a paralysis brought on when ideology replaces theology. When the very possibility of objective truth is deconstructed and immorality becomes a political crusade, atheism is ever more clearly an abstract form of ahumanism. Fashionable talk about having faith in yourself is unnecessary where there is faith in God who endows the self. When souls prefer willfulness over the freedom of the will functioning according to God's design, you may expect, and will certainly get, a crenelated ignorance of teachers and students. When that happens, God is not only banished from the neighborhood school and national university, mention of him becomes their only obscenity.

In the *Nicomachean Ethics*, Aristotle defined perfect happiness in intellectual activity as a free exercise of thought. That free exercise is guaranteed by the will obeying true laws. If "Idea" instead of God exhausts the definition of ultimate truth, the soul shrinks to its imaginative component, and its intellect and will quickly turn in on themselves, lying to the self and serving the self. The historic universities produced some of the most illustrious saints; they taught the ordering of the imagination along with the intellect and will in the search for God's truth. Supreme confidence in the humble use of the intellect moved Newman's vision of learning as fearless adventure, and this he unrolled sonorously in *The Idea of a University*: "The Catholic is sure, and nothing shall make him doubt, that if anything seems to be proved by astronomer, or geologist, or chronologist, or antiquarian, or ethnologist, in contradiction to the dogmas of faith, that point will eventually turn out, first not to be proved, or secondly, not contradictory, or thirdly, not contradictory to anything really revealed, but to something which had been confused with revelation." Universities have now become largely irrelevant to the integrity of the social order and, indeed, centers of social-intellectual confusion, by having lost the will to be what God wants them to be. A recovery of their social function will have to begin with a consideration of the meaning of sanctity. And this in turn will require affirmation of the resurrection of the dead as the hope of life and learning.

No adventure is more wrenching and at the same time more consistent with nature's true longing than being changed by God, and the ranks of the holy ones like Paul and Becket are evidence. But the change takes a will. And the change into eternal life requires union of the human will with the divine will. This is why Christ told the ruler to sell all he had and follow him. It was a moral test of the will; it was far more wrenching than a lesson in economic distribution. Faith is the ground of change by trusting the reason for change. The rich young ruler "became sad, for he was very rich" (Lk 18:23). He simply lacked the will to admit how poor his riches were making him through their artful illusion of permanence.

When our Lord effortlessly trumpeted that he was the resurrection, he immediately transposed the music of his voice and asked Martha quietly: "Do you believe this?" (Jn 11:26). Genesis began as the motive for such a moment, and Revelation is commentary on it. But if you want to see when it went to work in practical terms, you have to look at the Cross at the moment when the Good Thief moved his mouth and offered up his will in defiance of selfish logic and willful unbelief: "Jesus, remember me when you come in your kingly power" (Lk 23:42).

A Public Secret

There is in fact nothing secret about the way to eternal life. The Gospel is all about shouting the news on housetops and the danger of being deaf to the voice of the news. Secrets belong to the pyramids and occult desert tombs, and their legacy is one of finding the concealed passage and hidden door. Christ's body is a church and not a lodge. He publishes himself on the Cross, his flesh the poster on which the message is written.

The problem now is social censorship of the public fact, as it suppresses the call to holiness. In a world of complex definitions, it is quite amazing how literate people are speechless when it comes to defining a holy life. Holiness is the presence of God, and a holy human life is one that lives the virtues heroically as the result of Christ's own presence in the soul. It is the gift called sanctifying grace. And since man is not born with it the way he may be born with a talent or genius, he has to be reborn to receive it.

The goodness of the Good Thief on the cross was not intrinsic, for he was a thief. As a consequence of the original human rebellion against God's total honesty, all of us are thieves. "No one is good but God alone" (Mk 10:18; cf. Lk 18:19; Mt 19:17). Goodness is given by God, but man has to ask for it, and asking is the daring of humility. The plain fact learned from this unvarnished dialogue on the Cross is the availability of God to those who avail themselves of him. "Ask, and it will be given you; seek and you will find; knock and it will be opened to you" (Mt 7:7; cf. Rev 3:20). The asking has set in motion the greatest reforms in our brief human cavalcade. Godless revolutions are paltry blips on the political screen compared with the changes gained by souls simple enough to ask for eternal life. This was the defiant message Pope Pius XI smuggled past Fascist censors in march of 1937. He wrote in the encyclical *Mit Brennender Sorge* against the heartbreaking myth of immortal selfishness: "All true and permanent reform has in the last resort originated in sanctity, from men who were inflamed with the love of God and their neighbor, who by their great generosity in answering every appeal from God . . . have enlightened and renewed the times in which they lived."

Jerusalem fell, like other societies, from no crime louder than the closing of its shutters to God's appeals. If his quondam friends had not vacated the Way of the Cross, they would have heard him calling on them to ask for more than they wanted, to dare to ask for as much as he has to give.

When Christ was nailed between two guilty men, the options of free will for and against holiness were strung out for human view like a triptych. Its wood was the crosses, and the paint was sweat and blood; but the gold background was visible only to the conscience. One thief in the picture, helpless as a plucked chicken in a shop window, had his reasons for discounting the Perfect Man, rooted in disappointments and limited perception. But they were mock reasons. And, aided only by the quivering ends of his frayed ego, they rationalized the dialogue of man and God so that it became a mockery: "Are you not the Christ? Save yourself and us!" (Lk 23:39). The words spat from an alchemy of pain and hate became the diction for each succeeding age's attacks on the Christian fact, violent as the apostasy of Julian, neurotic as Bruno, vulgar as H. G. Wells.

On the other side of our Lord's Cross, and on the other hand of moral history, the Good Thief had no more particular understanding of Christ's supernatural identity. Where the other criminal had sarcastically called Jesus by his messianic title, the Good Thief was too delicate to embarrass the man in the middle with an honorific that might not be true. This is the only instance in the Gospel according to Luke when the Lord is addressed by name without some accompanying title. Jesus. Jesus, remember me. The Good Thief has used his reason as he could, but it has its limits. He has no more time for analysis or discourse or courtesies of address. His intelligence once served him well and perhaps so well that it began to disserve him into capital offenses. Now it is baked in a brain on fire. Jesus. The criminal's whisper is the plebiscite of the whole mangled pile of men who had found how it hurts to be human.

From his cross, two matchsticks in comparison with the monuments of antiquity, he looks in the face of the One on two other matchsticks. "A serene and placid countenance, that of a young man." At the same moment in Egypt, the face of Pharaoh looked that way hidden under a golden mask, and would look that way right up to now. One thinks of the kindly way the physician coming down the stairs of a country house in Surrey broke the news of the death of the sixty-four-year-old author of *Alice's Adventures in Wonderland*: "How wonderfully young your brother looks now." Youthfulness in death is the gift of living in the lands of endless youth. Pharaoh's young serenity and placidity had been through the courtesy of embalmers. Serene and placid through the courtesy of embalmers. But the eyes of Christ were of a living youth, alive as they are now, by the art of eternity and courtesy of divinity.

We could not even speak of these events were not those eyes on us at this moment. In the "eternal now" of his knowledge, his eyes watch man to see what man will see in him. He speaks with his eyes, glancing from ten thousand crosses over ten thousand altars, from the tiles of ten thousand mosaics and more thousands of statues, from the fleshless eyes of his Real Body in all the tabernacles of this absent-minded world. "Truly, I say to you, today you will be with me in Paradise" (Lk 23:43).

III

THE TEMPLE OF DIANA

"Woman, behold your son!" . . . *"Behold your mother!"*

The Symbol of the City

Ephesus, in what is now Turkey, was the fourth largest city of
the Roman Empire, and its proudest boast was to be care-
taker, or literally "temple-sweeper" (*neokoros*) of the Temple
of Diana, its symbol like the Eiffel Tower to Paris or the
soaring Arch to St. Louis. The fourth temple on the site, and
the one first officially remembered as a "Wonder", had been
completed in 430 B.C., after 120 years of construction, and,
measuring 425 feet by 220, was larger than St. Peter's in
Rome. A certain Herostratus set fire to it in 356 B.C., some
say on the very birth date of Alexander the Great, just to be
remembered by the ages, and by writing this we accidentally
help in some small way to honor his dishonorable intent.
The fifth temple was erected there around 330 B.C. from
designs of Chersiphron and his son Metagenes. They left a
building, it must be said, inferior in workmanship though
even larger than its predecessor, shimmering over the whit-
ened city and silty harbor of the blue Aegean, marble over-
laid with gold plates, enameled with scenes, decked with
gazing statues. The foundations would dwarf an American
football field, and its 106 columns stood five stories tall,
some a donation of the Lydian king Croesus, whose name
became synonymous with wealth.

To disgrace the Temple was to disgrace the city. But it was
more than a civic trademark. It was a copyright, and trades-
men made good livings selling copies of the Temple's high

goddess Diana, or Artemis as she was called by her Greek adopters, the fertility votive of Asia Minor, crowned with signs of the season and her bosom covered with breasts multiplied to nurse all who came to her.

If one of the sincerest traditions is true, the Virgin Mary came to this city in her last earthly years. And if she did, and if she refused to enter the Temple, she still must have noticed the miniatures of this garish figure on sale all along the way, like the little plastic Statues of Liberty with thermometers in their stomachs, on sale in Manhattan souvenir shops. Surely if she had lived for a while there, she would have been invited more than once to take in one of the Wonders of the World. And, even if she as a Jew found the goddess repugnant, she might have been urged to see the Temple's other marvel, a sacred stone dropped from Jupiter, probably a meteorite and rather like the stone the Muslims keep in the heart of Mecca. And as she refused these invitations, she may also have humbly reminded well-meaning guides that he who is mighty had done marvels for her and holy is his name. But the Ephesians were dead serious about their Dianas and placed them in areas of the Temple with endowments to keep them polished. On the annual celebration of her descent from Jupiter, a glittering parade of the shining dolls twisted through the streets to the open theatre.

On the Art of Shouting

Within no time after he arrived in Ephesus and began preaching, St. Paul started an uproar. Now this was for two reasons, and the second was the pompously raised complaint that he was bringing disgrace upon Diana, and thus on her temple, and therefore on the whole city. The first reason Paul's accusers thought of was more immediate and sincere:

in a city rather loose with name-calling, he who steals a purse steals everything. Paul was bad for business, and the business he was bad for was big.

Hostility to truth, one might think, is nurtured by love of lies, and this is so from a mental angle. The Ephesians, though, attacked Paul for the less cerebral reason usually lurking behind hostility to truth or even the suggestion of it: he was threatening their attachment to comfort. Many were the consolations from Diana's many breasts. She was the mother of sons who hated anyone who treated her poorly; she was also a rich mother whose heirs would kill anyone who made her poor.

Attachment to creaturely things is a natural animal affection. It becomes bestial when it is the governing affection in humans. Even St. Peter tottered on its brink when he betrayed his Savior to save his skin. There is a world of significance in the place where he did it: warming himself by the fire. Today a lazy mentality has raised warmth to an almost sacramental dignity. It is the psychology of Christians who have not had to suffer for their faith. They tend to think the finest compliment you can pay a church is to say it has "warmth"; and when they say a favorite priest shows warmth, which is a fine thing in itself, they can mean that he is not on fire.

The leader of the Ephesian artisans' revolt against Paul was the idol-maker Demetrius. He did not object theologically; his complaint was on flat and sensible economic grounds. What is good for the silversmiths is good for Ephesus. "Men, you know that from this business we have our wealth" (Acts 19:25). That was that. And it was effective enough to start a riot and a rally in the 25,000-seat public theatre to which they had dragged Paul's companions, Gaius and Aristarchus. So desperate was the scene, that Paul's companions would not let him go near. One fellow Jew, Alexander, tried to

defend Paul and those of "The Way", as Christianity knew
itself before it thought of itself as Christianity. Great things
can sometimes be on so vast a scale that they do not see
themselves. The Wonders of the World were wondered at,
but they were only called the Seven Wonders after some
time and from some distance. So it was too with the names
the Church used for herself and her bishops and her sacraments. The crowd, now a mob, shouted Alexander down for
two hours in the venerable tradition of mobs, and their cry
was: "Great is Artemis of the Ephesians!"

It was a grand-scale version of the preacher who wrote in
the margin of his pulpit text: "Weak point. Shout." And it
was a way of fusing confusion, for up to that point, "some
cried one thing, some another; for the assembly was in confusion, and most of them did not know why they had come
together" (Acts 19:32). There is not a political horror in all
history that cannot be traced back to some character who
appeared on the horizon with a catchphrase for people crazy
for something to shout together. Of course great prophets
have had their lines, too, and so there is the "Great Man"
theory of history. But with miserableness increasing to the
present, a stark light has been shed on the times by a "Bad
Man" theory. Diana had become Diana of the Demagogues,
and suddenly it became quite clear to the fractured crowd
what the formulaic response must be.

Nothing to Get Upset About

Then arrived that figure rarest in history texts and halls of
fame, but so numerous that he has come to be known as the
Common Man, who promotes the Great Man sometimes
unwittingly or even inadvertently and who confounds the
Bad Man sometimes the same way. The town clerk arrived

and said that there was nothing to get upset about: "Men of Ephesus, what man is there who does not know that the city of the Ephesians is temple keeper of the great Artemis, and of the sacred stone that fell from the sky? Seeing then that these things cannot be contradicted, you ought to be quiet and do nothing rash. For you have brought these men here who are neither sacrilegious nor blasphemers of our goddess" (Acts 19:35–37). The courts were open to Demetrius, and the craftsmen and proconsuls would hear them out. They should go home now or else risk arrest for rioting. Then the clerk dismissed the assembly with the unadorned dignity of the Common Man and, marvelous to say, the people went away, as suddenly and spontaneously as People's Governments melting away when the people stand up and simply tell them to go away, all to the astonishment of political scientists and journalists who know it cannot happen that way.

The town clerk was a master of crowd control. He was not a prophet. The Ephesian cult was not inviolable. It was contradicted by a glorious burst of true news by Paul to its shores, and it failed. Christianity is guaranteed to the end of time by the authority of God himself. But, let Christians first admit, the practice of Christianity is not guaranteed in any place. The gates of hell cannot prevail against the Church, but they can crush particular churches. Arid sands blow over the gritty ruins of once great churches in North Africa, as colder winds are blowing over remnants of churches in Western Europe and the cities of North America. Christ is forever; Christian culture is not. Thomas More wrote to his son-in-law, William Roper: "For as the sea will never surround and overwhelm all the land, yet it has eaten it in many places, and swallowed whole countries up and made many places sea, which sometime were well-inhabited lands, and lost part of its own possession again in other places, so, though the faith of Christ shall never be overwhelmed with heresy, or the gates of hall prevail against Christ's Church, yet as in some places it winneth in new peoples, so by negligence in some places the old may be lost."

It is not enough to say that we are a Christian people because we call ourselves Christians, or that we have nothing to fear of oppression because no one is taking away our churches. We can simply let them fall away, and they will go. An entire generation has grown up so influenced by the idolatries of television and aimless educators that they are little better informed of heaven and hell and all in between than were the smug Ephesians with their silver dolls and magic stones dropped from the sky.

Complacency is a corrosive spiritual failing, whose morbid slogan in the face of evil is, "It can't happen here." It is like the rare disease that deadens the sense of pain. This would be the most desirable of ailments were it not for the fact that pain can function as a warning signal, and without it one could die of unheralded malignancies. When the consciences of Christians are anesthetized by creaturely comforts, they do not feel the rot within. At the beginning of this century, Charles Péguy had already diagnosed it: "It is an un-Christian world, de-Christianized, absolutely totally un-Christian. . . . This is what the ecclesiastics do not see, refuse to see." The Ephesians refused to see that what was threatening them was more than an economic or civic danger; their whole religion and way of life were on the line, as they are with ours.

The enormous difference, of course, is that the Ephesian cult was false and the Gospel is true. Smash an idol and you get a broken idol; smash Christ and you get a broken world. The smashing can be a subtle habit, done by the velvet hammer of compromise, indifference, relativism and the selfishness that asks, not "Is this true?", but rather "What's in it for me?" If my works open me to the dangers of hell, then pretend, as a prominent politician recently declared, that the Second Vatican Council abolished hell. This is the philosophizing of the comfortable: the rationalizing of those who replace "I think" with "I feel" and who, instead of saying "I disagree", say "I'm not comfortable with that." We can feel comfortable by a warm fire, so comfortable that we lose sight of the truth and let the Liar of the World make the flames larger until they become hell. Christ's own earthly governor was governed by his feelings, and when he asked for a definition of truth he was too discomforted to wait for the answer.

A Great Wonder in Heaven

The legend of Diana-Artemis had her the daughter of Jupiter and Latona, born along with the handsome god of music, poetry, prophecy and medicine, Apollo. Her legend was drawn from numerous sources, as is evident from her various names and identities. As Ilithyia or Lucina to the Romans, she presided over childbirth; as a metaphoric Trivia, she was goddess of the crossroads where her shrines were erected to protect the trivial conversations and commerce of these meeting places; and she was goddess of the moon, and of virginity as well as the hunt.

Here the contrasts abound. First, the Lady who may have entered Ephesus after the Crucifixion had presided over childbirth too. The Lady of Legend was called the goddess; the Lady of Fact was one who bore the Christ, the Lord of Life. God. In the flagrant vulgarity of that time and place, whole populations had been fixated on the many silvered breasts of their nursing Diana, and the crassness of her charms reflected the immaturity of those who ogled her like a voluptuary on a modern rock video. The breasts of Mary were human and had been blessed by humans for having given milk to so wise and good a man, the same man some now were nursing with vinegar on the Cross while the Mother watched in agony.

Second, Mary had her own role at the crossroads. The whole idea of a god on a cross at the crossroads was foolishness to the abstract Greeks, as St. Paul found out the hard way, by trying to preach to them. But it was not a trivial idea, and Mary knew it. She began to know it for nine months within her being, and she followed the fact each step of the way to the Cross. For the Cross was more than it was for others crucified; the Son of God made it mark the crossroads of the world. For three hours the Woman stood at its base with the future Bishop of Ephesus, while the rest of the world had gone astray in trivial chatter, no Goddess of the Crossroads yet Mother of the Strays.

The third contrast is understood by moonlight. Where Diana had been goddess of the moon through whom the moon's glow lazily glided to those below, Mary was wrapped in a turmoil of light, like the flying folds of a bronze baroque statue. The apparent calm incandescence of the moon is in fact the loveliest of derivatives with no light of its own, and the loveliest Lady is the one who reflects no sun but the turbulent light of her one true Son. He will wrap her in an office and dignity by making her Queen of the Apostles and Mother of his Church. And as these carry no weight in terms of self-importance, and make sense only to those who take themselves lightly, they are worn by her as lightly as the light itself: "And there appeared a great wonder in heaven; a woman clothed with the sun, and the moon under her feet, and upon her head a crown of twelve stars" (Rev 12:1).

The Heart of Heresies

Heresies have been multiple and countless as the Church has increased her preachers to preach numberless times, for wherever their truth is heard it will be misunderstood by ignorance and distorted by pride. Those heresies catalogued and responded to in the manuals and those that lie in secret corners of anonymous minds, are nervous notes of one massive dissonance, bad articulations of one great speech and bad playings of one grand song. All heresies are modes of The Heresy.

The Word was made flesh through a womb, and he is twisted by thoughts and crucified by hands when that one womb is misunderstood. This is The Heresy. Every heresy about God is a heresy against Mary. It can come by the contempt of underestimation (as when she was forgotten at the Cross) or, more rarely, from the extravagance of distortion (as when immoderate and undisciplined spirits want to reduce her dignity to that of a Diana). It is not a matter of striking a balance between too little and too great honor, for of honor she could never have too little; the lowliness of the handmaid is precisely what God has looked upon, and she could never have too much honor in light of what her littleness reflects. Imagine saying to Christ: "I love you, but I do not love your mother."

St. Louis de Montfort says in *True Devotion to Mary*, "This is the reason why the reprobate, such as heretics, schismatics and others, who hate our Blessed Lady or regard her with contempt and indifference, have not God for their Father, however much they boast of it, simply because they have not Mary for their Mother." As she is the greatest one of our species, we get ourselves wrong either when we confine her to the obligatory Christmas pageant with children dressed as sheep, or when we caricature her as a gaudy allegory suitable for the Ephesian Temple. So it is inaccurate, and deadly for human identity, to make her into some sort of monarch, while insisting that as monarchs go she is only constitutional.

To speak of a dignity that can be too little or too much is to have entered the wrong terrain. Degrees of dignity are irrelevant when the essential dignity in her case is her relationship. She is a mother, and the question is not how often a son should call her a mother; the one relevant question is the identity of her son. A mother can be overbearing to her child, and a mother can be overborne by her child, but a mother cannot overbear her child. What Mary is, and by derivation, what all lesser humans are, depends on whom she has borne. And when that is answered, what matters is no longer her honors but her holiness. Holiness has its own etiquette and by it honors are as spontaneous and appropriate from the humble as they are affected and clumsy from the proud. It may be that the Blessed Mother appears more frequently to untutored children who doff their caps without thinking; people not used to being outranked would be too distracted.

Behold Your Mother

Four centuries after St. Paul caused his commotion, the bishops held a council, in 431, in the same Ephesus, and worked out a proper title for Mary. The Christians knew that, as Christ is the Second Person of the Holy Trinity and thus God, Mary, who is the Mother of Christ, is by ordered logic the Mother of God. At the same time she could not be the mother of the Eternal Trinity, since she is only human and not eternal.

Diana was a wonder of the world no longer; her memory was an embarrassment, and this was actually part of the problem. The problem was only a problem theologically, because the unity of the Trinity resists the neat tailoring of human analogies. If it did oblige analogy, it would only be analogous itself, and so the Christians known as Nestorians objected. Mary's title was a deeper problem emotionally, because the memory of a goddess hung like a bad dream over the city, even though in the first century Ignatius had spoken of the Mother of God, Theotokos, precisely by that title, as Origen had in the third and Athanasius in the fourth, and then Augustine Latinized it in the fifth. The freer translation *Dei Genetrix*, literally Mother of God, was even more violent to the minds of the Nestorians than the literal equivalent *Deipara*, or God-bearer, but it was the same in fact if not in emphasis.

The Nestorian prejudice belonged to the school of humanism that shies from anything so manly as the God-Man. It is as perennial in the hollows of the human psyche as moss is in the shade. Within lines of reference so instinctively narrow, the supernatural mystery of the divine enfleshment had to be a superhuman fantasy. Diana was a germ too long in the air to trust that she had been eradicated. The faintest language of the old days might bring back her slick altars and rancid incense. And of course there were others ready to prey on this caution. There were those who, when you got right down to it, denied the divinity of Christ except as a figure of speech, and they knew that the question of motherhood was inseparable from the question of the son's godhood. And in this they were more forthright than those since then who would have Christianity on their own terms apart from the Councils and Christ's own words from the Cross, who do speak of Jesus without speaking the way he spoke of his Mother. The motherhood may be ignored, as one may ignore the image on the obverse of a sheet of paper, but it cannot be detached from the fact of

Christ any more than one side of the same page may be detached from the other.

God plans things, and he planned Ephesus as the place to thrash this out. The site of the Council of Ephesus in 431 was almost certainly a church, the double church whose ruins remain, cheek by jowl with the theatre where the town clerk had confronted Demetrius and his howling retinue. The Temple of Diana had been reduced to its foundations in 262 by the Goths, whose ways were so wild that a non-Romanesque style of architecture would someday be named after them as an insult. Some of the assembling bishops must have studied the remaining columns lying like elephant relics; after the edict of Theodosius in 381, which formally shut all pagan shrines and grounds, a few of the pieces would eventually be installed in temples of the God whom Paul had proclaimed in those frenzied days at Ephesus. They are said to be the green jasper columns supporting the dome of Santa Sophia in Istanbul, and two stand in the cathedral of Pisa. Having a Council in the former home of Diana was more than an irony. It was very much what we might presume to call an extravagant gesture of Providence, and that is what we have to call it when we are too reserved to say heaven has its own hilarity. Sometimes this orchestrates felicitously, as when choirs of modern denominations that have pretty much ignored the Mother of God innocently sing the words of a favorite hymn: "O higher than the cherubim, More glorious than the seraphim. . . . Thou bearer of the eternal Word, most gracious magnify the Lord." To remain oblivious to the meaning of those lines, of Athelstan Riley inspired by ancient texts, is to live detached from the Council of Ephesus and thus to censor one of the acts of the Holy Spirit.

At the beginning of this century in England, a woman in the rural village of Sandringham was walking along the road carrying a heavy parcel when a large and sputtering machine called a motorcar drove up and stopped. The man in the rear seat apologized because he was traveling the other way and could not give her a lift, but would she accept a small picture of his mother? At first it was the last thing she needed, but the arm reached out and handed her a gold sovereign. Then drove off in the fumes of petrol and a good cigar the King of Great Britain and Ireland and Emperor of India. Two thousand years ago, the King of Everything spoke from the Cross and asked the world to accept a picture of his Mother. This was the final work he had to do on earth and the summit of what he had to do on the hill; there was nothing incidental about it, for it was the efficient signal that only now was his work done, and he cried out the meaning from his sharpest pain: To miss that, or to underestimate that, is to remain on the margin of God's plan for the world. There are no afterthoughts in a crucifixion; Christ's command to look at the Mother of God was his crowning sermon to creation, and his work was not done until he had spoken it.

> When Jesus saw his mother, and the disciple whom he loved standing near, he said to his mother, "Woman, behold your son!" Then he said to the disciple, "Behold your mother!" And from that hour the disciple took her to his own home. After this Jesus, knowing that all was now finished . . . (Jn 19:25–28).

Paganism and the Woman

As our Lord would not have saved an unimportant thought for so climactic a moment, I should not be surprised if the concept of the Mother of God makes me uncomfortable. Nor should I be surprised by the primary concept of the

Woman. Our Lord spoke of these things in the world's most important hours. That fact alone should rivet the world's attention. But when the world is like ancient Ephesus, preferring agreeable gods and profits, then it will reject the mystery of Mary for the same reason it should be acknowledged. It will say of the Motherhood of God exactly what Demetrius and his silversmiths said of the new Gospel arriving on their shores: not "I don't believe that" or "I can't believe that", but "I'm not comfortable with that."

The two most comfortable forms of religious speculation are paganism, which is a form of nonchalance about divinity, and pantheism, which is a form of laziness about divinity. Neither was able to make an association between divinity and holiness. At least Diana saved her clients from pantheistic indifference. But she was a dangerous illusion in spite of that. The divinization of fertility is a gentle way of demonizing it and makes the nurse a poisoner. Diana meant that nature is not divine but the nurturer is. Once life is detached from dependence on the Creator of life, it becomes a morbid fantasy, like the ghost of an amputated limb. Paganism saw the whole world filled with such shades and called them gods. It was tantamount to calling paintings the painter. But what makes the gods curiosities then is also what makes them freakish. The statues of Diana were like that, and, because divinity was imputed to them, their multiple breasts became ludicrous and not at all marvelous like the many eyes of the beasts in the Apocalypse who look to God. Quite the opposite, pictures of the Blessed Mother are less esoteric the more they illustrate her holiness. She is the perfect contradiction of the pagan silliness about nature.

Anyone can follow fashion and label the Christian understanding of women as stereotype imposed by a patriarchal society; and as with all things fashionable, the labeling is soon dated. It has been outdated by every age. If anything was ever consistent in the human experience of God, it was the way women kept the patriarchs from worshipping goddesses, and the spontaneity with which men flocked to shrines of the goddess in matriarchal societies. The entire line of women from Sarah and Rachel through Catherine of Siena and Isabella of Spain proves that, and it is vivid too outside that line of grace in the rhetoric of Hypatia and the war cries of Boadicea.

Where stereotypes exist, they belong to pagans and pantheists. But the Blessed Virgin is a radical and original understanding of God and his creation. From the Cross, our Lord addresses the Woman before the Mother, rooting her significance in primeval categories as prelude to historical categories of biological and spiritual maternity. The problematic Anne Emmerich claimed a private vision of the Woman: "I witnessed the soaring of her soul toward Jesus, who thought of her and who cast a glance at her as if looking for help. . . ." In his distress, incarnate Wisdom defies the neurotic human urge to go back to the womb; he reverts instead to the source of the human story, where the Woman cancels the loneliness of the Man even before she gives birth to others. Before calling Mary by the Aramaic "*Imma*", Mother, Christ addresses her as "*Itta*," "woman", as he had addressed the mother of a sick girl (Mt 15:28), the invalid (Lk 13:12), the bigamist (Jn 4:21) and the penitent (Jn 20:13). Mary is the Woman even before she is the Virgin Mother. By the strength of her immaculate freedom from original sin, a dignity of her own conception in preparation for the conception of Christ, Mary has a representative totality of all the broken world's parts.

Sinful woman's pagan temptation is to hide from the objective reality of the Creator, the God Without, and to console only herself with the autonomous illusion of the nurturer of life as the initiator of life; the temptation to hide from God by "unleashing the Goddess Within". Ordinary human sentiment may find that lush cultic fantasy comfortable and controllable and outside the challenges of the order of justice. Thus paganism, as a type of immaturity about creation, readily appeals to women suffering from arrested psychological development. And the "unleashed goddess" seeks equally immature men as agents. In the modern pseudo-pagan revival, all sorts of cries circle in the hysterical whirlwind: identity crises, sexual liberation, gender confusion. The Crucified One crushes the pagan temptation with his cry "Woman!" Eve fell in order to become a goddess. The New Eve kicked off the dust of Eve and got up to become a woman. And the human race finds its place in the eternal design by calling on the New Eve as Mother.

Cultured Orphans

When the criterion for reality is comfort, sensually or intellectually, the world becomes a more comfortable place. It also becomes an orphanage. The Cross disappears, but vanishing with it is the Woman who stood by it. The consequence for culture would be unspeakable except for the way they are shouted daily by irrepressible statistics. Comfortable art turns pornographic, comfortable science designs only gadgets, comfortable music lyricizes bromides, comfortable liturgies flaunt sentimentality, and comfortable families disappear. In 1970, 40% of families in the United States had two parents and at least one child under eighteen years of age; ten years later the figure was down to 31%, and by 1990 it was 26%. More than half of all children born in our nation today are likely to live in a broken home. For two thousand years Christ Crucified has been crying, "Behold your mother!" Now society whimpers, "Behold your surrogate mother!" Christ gives Mary. The world gives Diana. And Diana is an idol.

On the twenty-fifth day of July 1968, the idol was smashed. In the encyclical *Humanae vitae*, Pope Paul VI summoned the faithful to use the entire soul, intellect and will, to dismantle the unnatural pretensions of the idol convenience, "since man cannot find true happiness—toward which he aspires with all his being—other than in respect of the laws written by God in his very nature, laws that he must observe with intelligence and love" (no. 31). By accounts, that Pope was a man not enamored of controversy, eager not to mock the diction of thinkers whose thoughts were not his own, instinctively accommodating in secondary matters, solicitous of the weak by lessening their obligations, unconsoled in having to make final judgments and not hasty to give the rod sway when the staff went unheeded. *Humanae vitae* contained no new revelation, for there are no new revelations after Christ, and only etched more clearly what had been written by nature in the human heart. But it did show the effects of grace on the Pope's personality, for his native dispositions yielded to divine inspiration when he promulgated that most prophetic universal letter. When he did, the whole world sounded like pagan Ephesus invaded, and the howl against Paul VI amplified through nineteen centuries the outcry of the idol-makers against the first apostle Paul.

There were then, and still are, people like the smug town clerk who try to calm things by a municipal assurance against the need for violent opposition since this was so obviously a mistake that no one will believe it, and it will soon pass away. The people will vote with their feet, so there is no need to vote with fists. What really matters is our quality of life and our bond rating.

Did Paul VI make a mistake? In retrospect, his anticipation of "conjugal infidelity and the general lowering of morality" may be understated, but it is certainly not wrong. Nor can anything mistaken be found in his warning that "the man, growing used to the employment of anti-conceptive practices, may finally lose respect for the woman and, no longer caring for her physical and psychological equilibrium, may come to the point of considering her as a mere instrument of selfish enjoyment, and no longer as his respected and beloved companion." The entire point is missed by thinking that the Church requires women to be mothers; the Church is the unique voice in the world demanding that mothers realize why they are women. Were they to forget, a ghastly amnesia would erase the collective social conscience, and they would not be able to remind men why they are men. Those who had already forgotten these things hoped contraception would give birth to Utopia, the place that by definition is not a place. They will have to show how they were more prophetic than these words:

> Let it be considered also that a dangerous weapon would thus be placed in the hands of those public authorities who take no heed of moral exigencies. Who could blame a government for applying to the solution of the problems of the community those means acknowledged to be licit for married couples in the solution of a family problem? Who will stop rulers from favoring, from even imposing upon their peoples, if they were to consider it necessary, the method of contraception they judge to be most efficacious? In such a way men, wishing to avoid individual, family or social difficulties encountered in the observance of the divine law, would reach the point of placing at the mercy of the intervention of public authorities the most personal and most reserved sector of conjugal intimacy. (no. 17)

It is true that this warning has largely gone unheeded. It is also true that in these years since 1968 there have been a doubling of the divorce rate, a tripling of incidents of child abuse and violent crimes, a quadrupling of sexually transmitted diseases and a universal plague of abortions. We are back to the unlearned moral of Ephesus: smash an idol and you get a broken idol, smash Christ and you get a broken world.

With stunning impunity, the devotees of convenience try to preserve their cult with a new copy of their idol named "Safe Sex". Having defied the natural law only to meet the implacable resistance of natural effects, the Brave New World now scrambles for safety. Safety is not an inspiration. There has never been a safe symphony that endured, never a safe genius that invented, never a safe crusade that won. Beauty, truth and goodness imperil complacency; there is nothing safe about them.

Christ promises no safety and only a cross, but that ugly contraption is the machinery of the beautiful, the true and the good. The True Consoler told the fishermen to put down their nets and follow him. He offered no pension plan, he did not give the wedding couple at Cana a premarital agreement, and he did not give his Mother at the foot of the Cross a golden parachute. But hard hearts want soft words. And they are waiting to be whispered at every turn and crisis. The false Consoler watches for his Contradiction to leave with his cumbersome Cross, and then he speaks up. Each favor he offers is safe, the heart itself he makes a safe-deposit box, and he even packages an item he says is safe sex. Safety is Satan's habit and ritual incantation. It was the promise he offered Christ in three tempting ways in the wilderness. "I speak of peace while covert enmity under the smile of safety rules the world" (*Henry IV*, part II, intro. 9–10).

All that God gives in time is dangerous because all is handed still hot with the splendor of eternity, and the single way to handle his timeless gifts in fragile time without their singeing the self is with humility, for humility is docility to eternity. It is self-destructive to pretend that the moral obligations imposed by the gift of natural law are subject to our private conscience. The conscience does command our first obedience, and for that reason Newman called it "the aboriginal vicar of Christ", but it is only vicar and not Christ.

A Pope is responsible for teaching the truth because he is the immediate vicar of Christ. Thus Newman also says that conscience has rights because it has duties; these include the duty to be formed by the teaching of Christ through the Pope and the bishops in communion with him. The conscience contradicts its nature when it contradicts that formation. When, for example, Martin Luther took his stand saying, "Ich kann nicht anders", his analysis of the situation turned bravery into bravado. He could have done other, and he did not. Luther was taught such reverence for conscience by his Catholic teachers; he parted from the logic of the teaching by giving autonomy to private conscience. The mind may think a true thing, but nothing becomes true for having been thought. Pigs do not fly; pigs do not even fly when we sincerely think they can.

Private consciences are conscientious when they act according to an instinct for the good and the true, or according to what the Scholastics knew as *synderesis*. But even when consciences recognize, bear witness and judge, they do not become good and true unless they arrive at goodness and truth. Private conscience is merely subjective until it attains to the objective reality of public conscience. Now, public conscience is public because it is independent of private perception, not because it is acknowledged by any majority. Private conscience is really subjective conscience and thus can be ambiguous; public conscience is objective and thus certain. The Church as the Body of Christ is the vehicle of public conscience. When the Pope speaks infallibly, or requires the obedient assent of faith in his ordinary teaching, external commentators may think him arrogant; he is simply doing the humblest of acts, submitting himself and his own opinions to the way God has handed the truth on to this period of human experience. In the Pope's case, the "royal we" is a sternly humbling we, subordinating the Pope and all others to the notion of a mighty wind greater than the world itself. By the absolute will of the Christ of Galilee, the Pope stands in Rome and can do no other. If that compromises freedom of consciences, then every midwife compromises freedom of consciences by obliging the baby to open its eyes. From the Cross, our Lord told us that Mary would be the Mother of the Church, severe in a mother's love in guiding consciences into the world from the womb.

Authentic exercise of public conscience is the integral life of the Church. Basically, there is no difference between saying you must follow your own conscience and saying you must choose what is morally good. The only reason conscience is mentioned at all is to highlight the fallibility of private judgment and the need to discipline subjectivism in order to judge objectively. To hear some subjectivists, the expression "*sentire cum Ecclesia*", to think with the Church, means to stop thinking. It really means to think on the vastest scale with the boldest certitude.

The saddest chimera in response to *Humanae vitae* has been the misapplication of conscience as an excuse for disobeying a law intrinsic to nature: "I can do what I want with my own conscience." You might as well say, "I can sleep no matter who wants to wake me up." Any romantic can "dream the impossible dream"; it takes a special heroism to awaken from impossible dreams and do the possible. Confusion of private conscience with personal opinion was worsened by the lack of reinforcements and catechesis in the years following *Humanae vitae*. But as Leo XIII taught in his encyclical *Libertas praestantissimum*, and as Pius XI reiterated, freedom attaches to consciences, not to the conscience itself. Freedom of consciences is the human right not to be coerced in religious matters; freedom of conscience is an unreal claim to independence from the demands made by any law of God or man. Moral freedom is rooted in the free act of the individual person to obey the public facts of reality. These are not the same as public perception of reality. Even moral facts, which can be understood without the virtue of faith, can be widely misunderstood. So the Church instructs in natural law just as she instructs in revealed doctrines, though in the instance of natural law she need only explain and does not have to define.

The capacity of consciences for freedom is realized when they conclude in what the universal conscience of the Church has been inspired to teach. Were the Church "it", and nothing but an institution, "it" would be arbitrarily didactic and "its" wisdom would be like the rabbinical debates in the porches of earthly Jerusalem. Because the Church is "she", a life-giving mother, she is the means of freedom by virtue of an authority higher than her earthly licenses and systems: the Church is "Jerusalem from on high, which is free, our mother" (Gal 4:26). Conscience is never conscientious when it is isolated and accountable only to the self; then it would be a pseudo-science but not a conscience. I can follow my own conscience. I may not follow it wherever I want. Should pride persuade me that what I can do is what I should do, or that I cannot do what I do not want to do, I will follow my own conscience straight to hell.

Mary the Teacher

Mary was perfectly humble through her Immaculate Conception, and so only Mary had a perfect conscience. Consciences must be formed to obey the truth, and the question for our day is, Who will form them? When moral acts are only subjective functions and moral truths are only subjective perceptions, moral laws at best will be attempts to coordinate multiple opinions. When that happens, opinion polls and legislatures and courts replace the Church as moral teacher. Our generation has seen the collapse of the criminal misinformation of Marxism, but, in the practical atheism of any materialist culture, Etienne Gilson's caution is profound: "If we do not want to awaken some morning on the wrong side of the Iron Curtain, then we ought all to be interested in not letting the liberal State believe that it can indefinitely persist in educating children in view of nothing." The Berlin Wall has fallen, but the fictitious Wall of Separation between Church and State still is conjured as an excuse for education in moral slavery. In June of 1991, the Holy Father warned the people of Poland standing on the ruins of Marxism that they had to choose between civilization and anti-civilization, between a culture and an anti-culture. "And what should be the criteria of Europeanism? Freedom? What kind of freedom? The freedom to take the life of unborn children?"

Mary is the living conscience endowed to us from the Cross, singular in her obedience to the will of the Holy Spirit who leads into all truth. If the private conscience would be formed by the public opinion, it has indicted the conscience of Mary. If the liberal state is right, she is wrong. What then are her crimes? For if her obedience is wrong, and our pride is right, justice demands that she at least be informed of the charges against her. In Suetonius' life of

Caligula is a secular corroboration of the custom described in the Passion of Christ: the charges against convicts sentenced to the cross were written on a placard and carried before them or hung around their necks. It was done to Christ. It is done morally to his Mother. No one has grounds in justice to disobey the laws taught by God, without openly telling why the Mother of God was wrong in obeying them. She has been watching what we do with our consciences: "Mother, behold your son." Now we are free in conscience to judge her: "Behold your mother."

Who is to judge her if we do not? The liberal state has already passed judgment and found her mistaken about the holiness of life from the first moment of conception. In a recent summer in New York City a man killed and dismembered his six-day-old child and fed him to his dog. Horrified as the newspapers professed to be by this sensation, no one pointed out that the courts of our land would not have even accused the man of a crime if he had done the same thing seven days earlier. Yet such is the social order and atrophied historical conscience that now claims the right to form our consciences in establishing when life begins and when it should end and how to play it safe.

This ultimate issue of life itself will be either the destruction or revival of the present social order. And if it is to be revived, the new life will come through the littlest form of life, if only by their silent reproach to society's guilt. The legend of the founding of Mont-Saint-Michel in France is a metaphor. Early in the eighth century, the Bishop of Avranches, St. Aubert, wanted to build a shrine to the Archangel Michael on the site of a pagan monument, but the last stone of the old temple was too heavy to overturn. The men of the area were ordered to bring their sons, but they were not help enough. The bishop asked if all had been brought, and the father of sixteen admitted that he had left one home, but he was an infant. "Bring him!" bellowed the Bishop, and when that saint placed the child's tiny foot against the stone, the whole pagan edifice fell. By God's grace, the great stones of pagan pride in our society can be overturned. Each offense against natural law and the dignity of life can be overturned. Great men and women with learned voices and worthy example will lead the way; but the final stone will be overturned by a mother's baby. Each baby is the conscience of a culture. And when the last stone falls and a Christian age begins to flower, the crowds will no longer scream "Great is Diana of the Ephesians!" A newer song will be raised to the Mother of God and our Mother: "Hail, Mary, full of grace!"

IV

THE HANGING GARDENS OF BABYLON

"My God, my God, why hast thou forsaken me?"

A Maddening Splendor

The Semitic empire of Babylonia was founded about seven hundred years before its ruler Hammurabi codified a system of laws, and he did that some twenty-one hundred years before Christ came to earth and subjected himself to human laws. As empires tend to do, the Babylonian Empire had its ups and downs, but when it was greatest it stretched from the Persian Gulf to the Mediterranean, covering what we now call Iraq, Kuwait, Jordan, Syria and even Israel. It has taken a recent war to teach us some of that geography, and it has taken current politics to remind us that long before now there were rulers whose fortunes were as meteoric as their empires. Nebuchadnezzar II, for instance, was humbled at the height of his power, which he wielded from the city of Babylon, whose name in Assyrian meant "Gate of the God", about sixty miles south of modern Baghdad. As he walked on the terraces of his palace boasting of his might, judgment came upon him, and "he was driven from among men, and ate grass like an ox, and his body was wet with the dew of heaven till his hair grew as long as eagles' feathers, and his nails were like birds' claws" (Dan 4:33).

This is apparently a quite accurate description of the social trauma afflicting that period around the year 600. Archeological evidence corroborates the narrative. When Nebuchadnezzar came to his senses a more recollect man, he continued to build. Politics and economics aside, the most significant factor in his strength as embellisher of Babylon was the magnificent and mundane discovery of glazed brick. Its durability was far greater than sun-dried brick and was the ancient equivalent of modern steel. In his glory days, Nebuchadnezzar dug the Libil-higalla Canal and restored others, and built the first stone bridge over the Euphrates. But nothing was as impressive as the glazed South Citadel, a complex of palaces that legend boasted had been flung up in fifteen days, along with the 288-foot Tower and the ceremonial street of Aibur Shabu lined with 120 statues of fantastically painted lions.

To top this, literally, and to please one of his wives, Amytis, a mountain princess homesick on the arid plains, he commanded the construction of one of the Wonders of the World, the Hanging Gardens. Impressive enough physically, some 400 feet square and 75 feet high, with some terraces reaching possibly to 300 feet, as indicated from excavations and from the testimony of the priest Berosus about 200 B.C., they were remarkable for the first use of vaults in Babylonian construction and their irrigation by a triple-shafted well, a chain pump and a system of screws operated around-the-clock. The present ruler of Iraq has offered the equivalent of one and a half million dollars to anyone who can solve the puzzle of how it all worked. But it did work, and its splendor inflated its owner's sense of himself to the point of temporary madness.

The Hanging Gardens of Babylon struck wide fancy for two reasons besides their clever engineering. First, they had the power of romance. They were said to be the home of the legendary Assyrian queen Semiramis, who had been abandoned as a child, nursed by doves and, after royal marriage, had flown from the palace in the shape of a dove into the ethereal and immortal lands. More important, they were gardens. While buildings announce that humans are greater than animals, who build on a small scale when they do build, a garden is the sign that humans are not animals at all. Beasts are of the forest, man is of the garden. Man is nothing if he is not more than himself, and he is more than himself when he can imagine beyond himself. The ultimate imagining is Paradise. The word comes from the Persian name for garden. Paradise is said to have had its roots in the region of the Hanging Gardens, at least somewhere between the Tigris and the Euphrates, when "the Lord planted a garden eastward in Eden" (Gen 2:8). That does not mean Paradise was precisely there, but it does mean that those acres had been home to some primeval intuition that eastward Eden was and can be.

Three Gardens

We are alive and what we are because of what happened in three gardens: the Garden of Eden—Paradise given; the Garden of Olives—Paradise lost; the Garden of the Resurrection—Paradise found. A mediaeval manuscript says, "The garden of Paradise withered, and Christ watered it with his precious blood." Here is a reverse literature, for poetic license yields to historical fact. Paradise was lost as definitely as a sock or a set of keys is lost, and real blood brought it back. Some say the blood brought it back. They mean the same: it cost God nothing and everything to give of his perfect self-sufficiency. Christ alone is capable of regaining Paradise, for he alone has the map of it planted in his divine Wisdom. When you lose something and decide that it is lost for good, the sane reaction is to say you can get on without it, and the human adventure is the account of how we have done precisely that. It has required every kind of science and art at the disposal of ingenuity and has been the stuff of what we take for granted as comedy and tragedy. All told, it still amounts to existence instead of living. Reformers have refined the ways of existing, but for life to be lived there has to be a force more potent, a power of recovery more definitive, and that is salvation. Human greatness manages to rescue the remnant of life; divine grace bestows life as it was intended in Paradise. Thus holy sanity hangs for dear life on the difference between vaccination and baptism.

In Babylon the garden was built by human hands and irrigated by human means, and its magnificent failure consisted in constructing Paradise as a human initiative. The ageless temptation characteristically takes this form. In Eden the Tempter's feast of illusion was of this design, proposing a Paradise made of human hands once they learn the blueprint of reality represented by the fruit of the tree in the midst of the Garden. "You will not die. For God knows that when you eat of it your eyes will be opened and you will be like God, knowing good and evil" (Gen 3:5). But this false knowledge is ignorance of the other tree in the Garden, the tree of life itself. As God will reveal to St. John, this is the tree that matters: "To him who conquers I will grant to eat of the tree of life, which is in the paradise of God" (Rev 2:7).

Sin, as St. Thomas Aquinas totaled its moral sum, turns away from God and toward creatures. The fantasy goes beyond affection for creatures, which is normal and willed by God, and locates itself in an affection that denies the reality of God as the Creator of creatures. Creatures then imagine themselves as autonomous. In the French Revolution the lunacy attained a bizarre refinement when the turning away from God was politically institutionalized, and at one point the government invited the governed to worship trees. The Garden of Eden had so withered that where the first humans looked to a tree as a means of divinizing themselves, the French philanthropists began to grab the tree as the world's remnant divinity itself, rather the way a drowning man will grab on to a log lighter than himself to save himself.

The illusion has been an intrinsic part of the modern romance, and a close cousin of the French experiment is the contemporary attempt to construct political parties around environmentalism as the cipher for civilization. The red flag of revolution has become the green flag of devolution, a philosophically naive surrender to pantheism under the guise of "creation spirituality". Or, more accurately, it is the agnostic version of pantheism known as pananimism and panpsychism, by which the West's first identified philosopher, Thales, around the same time Nebuchadnezzar was rebuilding Babylon, ascribed a soul to everything. However varied have been the modern reworkings of the pagan confusion, sentimentalization of American Indian religion being one case, red banners of materialism and green banners of pantheism are draped around the same gnarled tree that broke our first ancestors' hearts.

Halcyon overestimation of the unaided creaturely potential comes by a grotesque underestimation of the tension between good and evil. At fault is the shortness of human memory, which is not even as old as the human race. Satan has a much older memory, and his identity in fact is as the rememberer of the heaven he lost. And heaven is the fact of which the earthly paradise is the glimpse. Satan's memory is ugly gristle and a grisly emptiness that he cannot fill. His one recourse then is to spread its emptiness in humans, for they are the only creatures capable of losing or gaining the fullness of eternal life in heaven. The knowledge he uses as bait is essentially not objective awareness of good and evil; it is rather the conceit of being able to define good and evil on one's own terms. Our delicate teeth bite into that overripe fruit any time we say, "That may be true for you, but it's not true for me."

If there are passwords to get into a place, that is the password to get us out of the ultimate place called Paradise. And one is naive who thinks that this language is unreal for being clothed from the wardrobe of myth. If the false autonomy to redefine moral reality is real and moral reality unreal, then we have to delude ourselves into thinking that the rejection of God has made us gods. The illusion may be sustained within the pages of certain philosophical texts. But when we walk down the streets of our cities and are mocked by billboard advertisements of half-pleasures and by broken drug needles on the pavements and by the painted eyes of saddened faces, then perhaps reason can weep at least one tear as old as the first Man with his Woman when they crossed the line from Paradise to the Wilderness of the World.

Three Stages of Shame

As Adam hid from God when his fantasy was exposed, so does the proud soul become ashamed when dosed with moral reality. Shame is not a virtue. It is not to be confused with contrition for sin. Shame may be pride uncovered, and when it is, it passes through three typical stages. While part of the private human psyche, they mount the public platform as cultural trends. Depression, the first stage, has widely publicized itself in the form of "angst" in the arts and as sloth or moral indifferentism in philosophy. Anxiety is the initial response of the soul that is frustrated in its natural and proper human quest for happiness. "Man wills happiness of necessity; nor can he will not to be happy, or to be unhappy" (S. Th. I-II, 29, 3). When it is not recognized as a pathology, it has been admired as the very spirit and complexion of modernity. Thus Jacques Maritain in *Scholasticism and Politics*: "The most unhappy creature necessarily desires happiness, and no doubt that is why he is so unhappy; for his plight is such that, according to natural conditions, he is normally led to despair of ever reaching this happiness." In the modern account, this "angst" perversely postures as a proxy for happiness; despair becomes an end in itself, and even a good.

Commitment to the absurd gives the despairing soul its one semblance of life and curiosity. J. B. Priestly detected this as one of the three main themes of the avant garde, along with its uncertainty of identity and the difficulty, or even impossibility, of human communication. Some justify artistic despair by saying there is more to it than meets the eye. But when a culture begins to realize that there is nothing more to it than meets the eye, and perhaps less than that by moral counterfeit, then the shame moves into its second stage, that of anger. The poet John Berryman, not long before his suicide, gave voice to a large number of voiceless moderns when he said, "I'm cross with God who has wrecked this generation." And that part of an angry generation that does not destroy itself moves into the third stage of shame, by diverting its corrosive anger onto others through cruelty.

Sprawled large across the modern age, depression took gigantic shapes in nihilism and existentialism and materialism. Its most neurotic expression came when it said God is dead. It turned angry when the declaration proved as empty as Pilate's irascible decision to tack sarcasm on top of the Cross. Then the anger turned cruel. When you count the hundreds of millions killed in its wars and revolutions, the twentieth has ended up being the most brutal of centuries, and never crueler than when it feels superior to earlier inquisitors and torturers while ignoring the millions of innocent lives being destroyed by legal fiat and technical efficiency.

A recent traveling exhibition of Mexican art was a paradigm of the century's regress. For while it traced the development from pre-Columbian art with its themes of human sacrifice (which practice the guide book neglected to criticize) through the baroque age of the colonial Christian missions (whose theme of Christ's vicarious sacrifice the guide book neglected to praise), it ended with the modern art of the anti-clerical Revolution, full of the satanic imagery of Rivera and Siqueros, and the violence of Orozco's sinister palette: "I prefer black." The twentieth century had returned to the geometrical fangs and claws of pre-Columbian culture, when the Sun was "the cause of all" and the "precious water" ritually offered to it was blood, and war was a god named Huitzilopochtli who demanded the sacrifice of those captured in his wars. Revolution had not recovered an Eden of jade and gold. Revolution had surrendered to the jungle with roots entwined around the fine things of the earth.

All of this has one perfection, and that is its symmetry with the moral decline of Judas, who is as symbolic of man after the Fall as Adam is symbolic of the Fall itself. Judas passed through the three stages of shame with translucent calculation. In the stage of depression he roamed the streets of Jerusalem, bereft of hope. The amber walls glared at him in his fever. "Then", at the Last Supper, and because sadness is an ally of evil, "Satan entered into Judas called Iscariot, who was of the number of the twelve . . ." (Lk 22:3). Again, in the morbid typology of pride, self-justification took the form of anger against Christ, whom he had betrayed. And Judas plotted destruction, the aspiration "God is dead!" hot on his breath. Anger sharpened into cruelty as Judas kissed Jesus—a customary gesture of a student toward his rabbi.

Offended pride twisted the protocol, and a snarl on the lips of Judas branded Christ with a mark that had never before touched the Holy Face.

The twentieth century has kissed Christ with that mark. Each false attempt to build Paradise without God has burned cynicism on the Holy Face. Depressed, angry and cruel, the modern age has fallen into Akeldama, the field of blood, and the end of the age is all red (cf. Acts 1:19). Not the red banners of tyranny that are threadbare, and not the red lights of harlotry too sickly to glow, and not the red tape of bureaucracy tied up in itself. It is all red with its own blood spilled by its bloodless theorists, who promised a subjective happiness greater than the objective good of God as the ultimate end of life. So much for the modish paradise of the moderns. And until man alive recovers his grasp of reality, he will consort in spirit with the Babylonian king who built his garden and then was driven from among men to go mad in the dew of heaven. An aesthetic longing for nature unadorned, or a superstitious confidence in natural innocence, cannot cure that pathology.

The Fourth Temptation

Christ saves man by entering the withered garden and wrestling with cynicism in the most palpable presence of Satan himself. He penetrates the shattered Paradise, figured as the Garden of Olives, and begins the agony. The Greek *agonia* was a wrestling arena, and the arena of the Passion is the garden. Judas flung himself into Akeldama in surrender; Christ approaches the field of his own blood with courtly deliberation as for combat. Satan insinuates himself through depression, and, as he entered Judas in his depression, so now he would enter Christ by making him depressed. And the vehicle is the vampire philosophy of meaninglessness hollowing a hallowed heart.

This is the Fourth Temptation of Christ. At the beginning of the messianic preaching, Satan tempted our Lord three times in the wilderness, and after forty days, ". . . when the devil had ended every temptation, he departed from him until an opportune time" (Lk 4:13). The opportune time had come. After the three temptations in the desert, the fourth would come in a garden older than its ancient olive trees. "My soul is very sorrowful, even to death . . ." (Mt 26:38).

Preparations for this agony had been deliberate, like any formal duel: "Now is my soul troubled. And what shall I say? 'Father, save me from this hour'? No, for this purpose I have come to this hour" (Jn 12:27). To destroy the lazy beguilements of absurdity, Christ would have to pass through its prelude in the form of a depression dripping from the eaves of hell. When others have fallen into it, he would march against it. Even this most intimate moment is made public, more than the grimacing and anxiety of a professional athlete enlarged in close-up shots and televised across the nation. What is almost indecent is holy here, and the eye of history is not prurient for staring. Christ's own humility tears open his consciousness, like opening a clock to show its works or like a surgeon's clamps prying back reddened ribs to show a living heart. It was meant to be that way. "So, could you not watch with me one hour?" (Mt 26:40).

Heaven sends a single decency: as with the three earlier temptations, he was helped supernaturally. While in the desert the help came afterward as refreshment, in this the hardest of the temptations it came during the agony as between the rounds of a fight. He was strengthened by a creature so superior to human creatures that it has no need of reason. Its intellect was the transparency of heaven, and the creature was an angel (Lk 22:43).

God Forsaken by God

At this point a calm might have settled in, but instead crowds and a cross are dragged onto the scene, and their interplay prompts the degeneration of the holy city from depression to anger to cruelty. The ultimate cruelty will be the nerve-shattering horror of death at the third hour. But not before an engagement with anger, and Christ will sanctify it as he sanctified the holy depression in the Garden of Olives, and as he will sanctify the cruelty of the Cross with his last breath. Christ's anger comes after Mary has been bequeathed as Mother of the Church and utter solitude descends on Calvary. Here is a flagrant rendezvous with the absurd, and Satan has used all his temptations to prevent it. It is one anger he cannot exploit. Though he wants very much that we should encounter the anger of despair, because our weakness is susceptible to it, he desperately would keep Christ from it, because our Lord knows it is a mirage. Experience of it is hideous, nonetheless. But for the Truth to enter it is to call its bluff. He will cry out despair in a way that makes hypocrites shake with delicious pity, but nothing else shakes. The stars will not float down like confetti, and the sky will not fold up like a paper fan with nothing behind it. Only illusions are illusions, and Providence is not an illusion.

Jesus will endure the sense of abandonment by the Father, but, since the Father and he are one, that suffering has a power as constructive in him as it is destructive in us. At this moment, philosophy is supposed to enter from the wings of the twentieth century and cry out "God is dead!" And it does indeed sound like that from the Cross. But because the sound is a cry from God himself, it is the final fracture of that lie. "*Eli, Eli, lama sabachthani?*" "My God, my God, why hast thou forsaken me?" (Mt 27:46; cf. Mk 15:34). In the Gospel according to Matthew, Christ speaks some forty times to his Father. Here his lips form the unfamiliar address, "God", and thus he turns inside out every illusory revision of our heavenly Father as an abstraction. Once God the Father becomes abstract, moral life disintegrates as it is relocated in insubstantial concepts like "Society" and "The People" and "Progress". As the philosopher wrote, "A crowd has no hands." On Good Friday, one looks in vain for mankind in despair; a man despairs. In the crowd are individuals with hands; and the applause is sickening.

For a few moments, Christ makes himself an abstraction to confound modish abstractionism; he makes himself nothing to confound nihilism; he makes himself an object of scorn to confound scornful subjectivism. The Way loses his way so that wanderers might see it for the first time. The Truth imitates a lie so that liars might see the architecture of honesty. The Life declares his life abandoned so that mortals might measure the vaults of the will that willed us into life.

Abandonment cried out by the Beloved is a vaccine for the disease that looks at God and thinks it sees death. There is no need to translate the Fourth Word from the Cross; the evangelists found it so daunting that it must be kept in its own syntax. What matters is this: Christ died on the Cross to live again, and in so doing he made the sense of abandonment an act of recovery. Our dissonance is his hymn. Christ is the Truth alive, and when the Truth utters the ultimate absurdity of Modernism on the Cross, the absurd dies by its own absurdity.

The Scarecrow in the Garden

There is a scarecrow on Christ's Cross. This must be said with all reverence, since his disfigurement was all for our sake, shaped "like a root out of a dry ground; he had no form or comeliness that we should look at him, and no beauty that we should desire him" (Is 53:2). And it must be said with awe, because it was such a studied part of so meticulous a plan. When the world appears as a withered garden, Christ will hang in its midst to frighten away its destroyer. Nothing can frighten the Voice of Contradiction except the most contradictory of sounds: God's cry of fear with himself. We fear what we cannot see, and we cannot see light, we can see only what light shines on. A weak man is afraid of his own shadow; but when Christ becomes afraid of what seems to be a shadow within the Eternal Light, he is looking within himself, and the vision stirs its own ineffable strength. During the desolation of Christ, the Trinity is still a unity; Christ can do no wrong and he can get nothing wrong, and his impression of abandonment is not wrong even though he is not abandoned. Instead, it is the perfect symmetry of Christ's suffering with the human condition, tempted in every way we are, including that most pathetic temptation of life's meaninglessness. While sins are violations of reality, the state of sin itself is abandonment to absurdity. So Kierkegaard insisted that the opposite of sin is not virtue, but more precisely faith. By deliberately willing a test of faith, Christ robbed meaninglessness of its definition and permanently humiliated it. He shamed absurdity by exposing it on a tree, just as absurdity had shamed the first man in Paradise, who hid behind a tree. By making the torture of meaninglessness part of his Passion, Christ drew the marrow of banality out of its bone. The Passion on earth has an unearthly obedience, and the cry of dereliction gurgled in blood becomes an art of synchronized movement toward a great and happy good. To the problem of how Christ's suffering could be real if he knew it had a victorious purpose, this cry is the key.

These racking moments, which seem to offend the virtue of hope, are not sinful, for God in Christ cannot contradict himself by sinning. Rather than being made to sin, Christ is "made sin" itself, encountering the contradiction of God by which man fell. As he and the Father are one, the contradiction of God takes place within his own soul, and as he is God, the contradiction becomes nothing less than the affirmation of who he is and why he came into the world. The cry of abandonment by the Messiah who had been made sin is history's definitive act of hope: that is, God's hope in the willingness of his human children to fight alienation from his Providence. "We beseech you on behalf of Christ, be reconciled to God. For our sake he made him to be sin who knew no sin, so that in him we might become the righteousness of God" (2 Cor 5:20–21).

Since the Passion of Christ, the temptations to sadness and futility have not gone away, but no reason for them exists. "There is no fear in love, but perfect love casts out fear" (1 Jn 4:18). It is wonderful to think how these words were written by an old man who in his youth had stood at the foot of the Cross watching Love do just that, with nails in his flesh and an unbearable sorrow in his soul. Other men on crosses spat out fear, Christ cast it out. And when he did, he cast it directly into the twisted intelligence of Satan. In Gadara he had cast devils into swine, and now he casts swine into devils. This is the start of the harrowing of hell, and the words "*lama sabachthani*" begin the exorcism of the whole human race. The line, chosen with the acuity of divine intelligence from the Twenty-Second Psalm, began a song of triumph. And now the triumph takes on a deeper moral dimension, because the Son of God is voluntarily sharing a sadness with men who, since they had to leave the Garden of Eden, had thought God had been the one who made them sad.

The despair of Adam, the despair of the Jews in the wilderness, the despair of Absalom, the despair of David for Absalom, the despair of Job, the despair of Jeremiah had made Satan sing his monotone song all through their laments. Now the gasping of Christ drives Satan wild with fear. "*Eli, Eli, lama sabachthani?*" It explains how Christ "descended to hell" with bells on. It explains how the faintest decibels of his falling tears opened graves. The cry has power to frighten away the shadows that come into Paradise, and it is heard back in time as well as into the future. The cry carries back to the ears of Adam and the wandering Jews and Job and Jeremiah, at the same time it carries forward in time to console those who cry in violated wombs and bereaved households and beds of pain. And wherever God has been mocked in courtrooms and congresses and schools and chanceries and sacristies, it will be the terror of men quite as it terrorized the Satan of men on Good Friday. "Yet once more I will shake not only the earth but also the heavens" (Heb 12:26).

In the three hours of galvanized agony, our Lord becomes a bloody patchwork of mankind's foul deeds and fouler distresses. The world's isolated and disjointed agonies were assumed by him who allowed death to consume him. "*Vita et mors duello conflixere mirando*"—Life and Death in dreadful combat fought. His own soul became like that curious small patch of land in the battlefield of Verdun, the Mort Homme west of the Meuse, little more than the size of a vegetable garden, which saw such dreadful slaughter in the battle's unsurpassed carnage during the First World War. Guides approach it with reverence and even hesitation because of its silence, more intimidating than unexploded mines. Though trees have begun to grow there again, travel writers claim, like Keats in "La Belle Dame sans Merci", that no bird has nested in any branch, and the only sound is the whistling wind.

The vacancy in Verdun is a natural glimpse into the Fourth Word choked from the Cross. The sufferings of every battle fought since Cain struck Abel are not as great as the recapitulation of human existence in the Sacred Heart of the Perfect Man. He does not "foresee" the noisy concert of human agonizing through the ages so much as he "sees" it all at once and "feels" it all at once. When we try to comprehend that, we can partially understand how he knows what crimes will happen until the end of time without either compromising our freedom to commit them or being cruel in refusing to prevent them. They are the nails in him. He knows more of their pain than we do even when we suffer them, because he is pierced by them in one part of one day of history.

This is the suffering of the Christ of God who cannot suffer. Man who can suffer may not interrogate its reason or justice, and the sanity of man cannot rationalize it or judge it. "I have yet many things to say to you, but you cannot bear them now" (Jn 16:12). One thing he did say we can bear: "Just so, I tell you, there is joy before the angels of God over one sinner who repents" (Lk 15:10). As that is the case, reason and justice do have the nervous duty of asking how much sadness there must be before the angels of God when sinners look at the Cross and laugh as the Son of God cries.

A young immigrant couple from Eastern Europe said to an American priest: "You remind us of the priests back home, because you do not tell jokes in front of the Blessed Sacrament." An experience of suffering teaches reverence for the Passion and for the Eucharist that is the fruit born of the Tree of the Passion, a fruit as bidden as the fruit of Eden was forbidden. A nation unfamiliar with the life of the Cross is in danger of telling jokes in the presence of such holiness. The Eucharist is a celebration of a solemnity, a sacred dance too vast to be timed only by the human pulse.

There are fully grown and neatly coiffed adults who have forgotten that, if not willfully then by neglect. When they forget, they may chatter like insects before and after the Holy Sacrifice, and they may speak lightly during it as though at an entertainment. They may even applaud the choir and themselves when it is over. It should not be done. It does not participate in the Sacrifice; it participates in the laughter of the crowd when they heard Christ cry "*Eli!*" "All who see and mock me, they make mouths at me, they wag their heads" (Ps 22:7). There are myriad ways in which a soft and disinterested culture can detach itself from the Passion of Christ, through sloth or nonchalance or formalism or mediocrity. Each puts the modern crowd with the old crowd that said on that middle day of history: "Wait, let us see whether Elijah will come to save him" (Mt 27:49). The prophetic song begun tortuously by the Victim rhymed their smug superficiality: "He committed his cause to the Lord; let him deliver him,/ let him rescue him, for he delights in him!" (Ps 22:8).

The Hanging Gardener

Other gardeners design scarecrows from remnants at their disposal, from rags and refuse. To protect the heavenly garden, that is, eternal life, the scarecrow is the heavenly Gardener himself. The sacrifice and the Sacrificer are the same. "But when Christ appeared as a high priest of the good things that have come, then through the greater and more perfect tent (not made with hands, that is, not of this creation) he entered once for all into the Holy Place, taking not the blood of goats and calves but his own blood, thus securing an eternal redemption" (Heb 9:11–12).

He looks very much like a wrecked and discarded artifact as he is taken down from the Cross. The soldiers toss to the ground his cap of clotted thorns, where it remains until someone perhaps furtively collects it. A pattern has come full cycle: when Adam was expelled from Paradise he found the verdant land yielding to thistles and thorns, and now the Second Adam's own brow has borne their sharp vintage. When he rises on the third day, Mary Magdalen is not frightened as she might well be by a ragged remnant; she thinks he is a gardener. It is a magnificent mistake, and the kind of mistake that is not as misleading as a correct answer. Anyone who knows the long trail from the Garden of Paradise to the Garden of Olives knows that he is the Gardener more prosaically than poetically. As once he walked through Paradise in the cool of the evening and called to fallen Adam, now he walks through the Garden of the Resurrection in the cool of the dawn and calls to the absolved Magdalen. Magdalen, who loves the One who did not shame her, has no need to hide as did Adam, who was too ashamed to love. "Her sins, which are many, are forgiven, for she loved much; but he who is forgiven little, loves little" (Lk 7:47).

Chronic instances arise when even the life of grace may seem dry, those times when Paradise seems like a desert. "My strength is dried up like a potsherd, and my tongue cleaves to my jaws . . ." (Ps 22:15a, b). Aridity of spirit, temptations and suffering for faith in God are priceless misfortunes in the economy by which Paradise is regained only by experiencing Paradise Lost. Even in the desert small flowers appear, and their perfume is known to none but God. By an act of faith the soul can enter that wilderness. Through patient endurance and mortification of the passions, the soul can take delight in what delights God. The Cross is the way to the true garden. "Peace I leave with you; my peace I give to you; not as the world gives do I give to you. Let not your

hearts be troubled, neither let them be afraid. You heard me
say to you, 'I go away and I will come to you.' If you loved
me, you would have rejoiced, because I go to the Father; for
the Father is greater than I" (Jn 14:27–28). Artificial para-
dises flowering from false consolations can be as wonderful
as the Hanging Gardens in the ancient world. And like the
Hanging Gardens they lie in ruins when the claptrap
machinery that irrigates them, however clever, falls apart.
"Thou dost lay me in the dust of death" (Ps 22:15c).

The Hanging Gardener has won for his friends a more
glistening garden, at an infinitely great sacrifice. He moans as
he tries to sing the song: "I can count all my bones;/ they
stare and gloat over me;/ they divide my garments among
them,/ as for my raiment they cast lots" (Ps 22:17–18). Is it
hard to believe that we will wake up in more golden fields
because of his naked bones and blood? It probably would
not be true if it were easy to believe. There are words more
wonderful than pitiful human exegesis to assure the tentative
heart of man. If we do not understand fully why he spoke
them, or fully what he meant when he spoke them, we do
know who spoke them: "If God so clothes the grass of the
field, which today is alive and tomorrow is thrown into the
oven, will he not much more clothe you, O men of little
faith?" (Mt 6:30; Lk 12:28).

V

THE COLOSSUS OF RHODES

"I thirst."

What Rhodes Built

Roughly three hundred years before the Incarnation, the eastern Mediterranean had become a major merchant area and the Isle of Rhodes had staked its own primacy in the Aegean Sea. A romantic connection with its namesake, a nymph Rhoda, who was daughter of Neptune, was tempered by shrewdness when it came to governing the chartless waters. Rhodes owed much of its commercial prominence to the way it had succeeded in limiting piracy and establishing the equivalent of what would come to be known as an international law of the sea.

If patriotism is not enough, as Nurse Cavell said in the Belgian dawn, it still is something; it is a virtue. And when it becomes the last refuge of the scoundrel, at least the scoundrel is hiding within a virtue, as Dr. Johnson himself would surely have admitted. The Rhodians did a sensible thing and not a silly thing in the high pitch of patriotic pride, and that was to build an extravagant statue. They could have chosen a figure of one of their admirals or governors, which would have been preening; they chose instead one of their gods, the Roman Apollo, the god of light who had become identified with the Greek sun god Helios. An effigy of one of themselves would have been elegant self-advertising; to honor a god was a modest way of saying that Rhodes had been favored. One might take credit for a ship or for a fleet of ships or for the government that organized them and sent them forth and back, but one does not take credit for the sun. There are deeds to boast about; the sun is just to bask in. Allowing for some crotchety neo-classical prejudice, a man in the early nineteenth century named Thomas Peacock was not being altogether obscurantist when he wrote: "Ancient sculpture is the true school of modesty. But where the Greeks had modesty, we have cant; where they had anything that exalts, delights or adorns humanity, we have nothing but cant, cant, cant."

The statue was drafted by the sculptor Chares and stood on a promontory overlooking the harbor, a feat of engineering that took twelve years to complete, around 285 B.C. There it would pose all through the fulfilling of time and coming of Christ until toppled by so indignant a thing as an earthquake. Its bronze pieces would lie scattered on land and under the sea until the spirit of enterprise gathered and sold them to a Saracen scrap metal dealer in 656, when all the world to the west seemed to be falling apart and ready for the heap. And there would have been a lot of Apollo to sell; he had stood 105 feet tall, the burnished synonym for things colossal.

There is something whimsical at least about the figure of a man serving no purpose other than to loom over the water slightly bowlegged. It did in fact serve two purposes, and the first was to dramatize sea travel as a sign that the world was getting bigger and more exotic, exactly opposite the modern idea of air travel as a means for making the world smaller and more familiar. The second was to express the happiness of Rhodes in being Rhodes, even to the point of hilarity. A Colossus advertised that better than something more utilitarian because it had an element of sheer delight in itself. Though the classical Isle of Rhodes may not conjure in minds an immediate association with Trenton, New Jersey, that worthy city has a humbler version of the same idea. It is in the form of large letters on a bridge the train passes and so placed that you cannot miss the message: "TRENTON MAKES THE WORLD TAKES". The sentiment is just right. It would be less perfect if it were not mounted so audaciously. It would be less clarion if it read: "Trenton manufactures excellent products, and the international market purchases them." People satisfied with themselves may speak that way, but rhymes are for people positively happy with themselves.

Because the Colossus was meant to be huge more than to be a work of art, though like the statue of Zeus on Olympus it fit the beautiful canons, its flair had a dignity of its own, more like that of a large billboard that means to be a billboard and not a mural, or like a park designed as an amusement park rather than as a scientific botanical garden. And it must be said that Apollo was just the right god for combining grandeur and merriment, like combining the augustness of a caesar with the levity of the holiday month named for Caesar Augustus. He was flagrantly too much of a good thing, and even the stories about him had an element of farce: instance his heavenly archery games with Python, or Daphne turning into shrubbery to escape his panting pursuit. Chares was a genius, but anyone could have thought his Apollo garish in the sun. When you are being amused, garishness takes on a sublimity of its own. The god was not exactly, as the rash expression goes, god-awful, but its awesomeness was of a peculiar kind—the kind that makes the term "awful" ambiguous.

A Colossus rising over the sea was magnificent for its incongruity, like a plastic American garden gnome set up in the heart of Africa. In those well-proportioned times, there would have been critics who thought it tasteless, the way Horace Walpole thought Shakespeare "undoubtedly wanted taste", and it would have been were it meant as a funerary monument or a cenotaph for the valiant. But it was meant to look like it enjoyed being tickled by the sea and lapped by the sea's foam. It was vulgar only if the sea is vulgar by being too big or too loud. Later legend claimed the god's wide stance had straddled the whole roaring harbor. The Colossus stood, or rather posed, on his pedestal, mightily to be sure, yet with the mock seriousness of a man flexing his muscles to impress his girlfriend. Only this merry man was a god, and his merry harem was "the multitudinous seas incarnadine".

Christ on the Water

Apollo's imaginary power touched what might be some of the nicest occupations of human culture. Here we can rescue that word "nice" from the way it is commonly used to sound fatuous. Nice originally meant either innocent or ignorant, and if this distinction is just hair-splitting, then it was by this very hair's breadth that our first ancestors opened great gates to misery. But unfallen angels do not confuse innocence with ignorance, and so they speak lightly of innocently nice things the way they speak lightly of all the most awesome things. It is a way of paying tribute to the light itself, which is the strongest of God's creatures. Some of the nice things bright Apollo was god of, besides the light, were poetry, music, prophecy and medicine. The Deceiver of the human race abhors innocence, and so he hates nice things like rhymes and harmony and narratives and prescriptions. First of all he hates the first nice thing God made, which is the light, and he takes pleasure in watching it burn fields and flesh. He is pleased, too, when poetry rhymes nonsense, when music is sour, when narratives grow dull and medicine poisons. The terrible beauty of niceness turns terribly ugly when it loses its innocence and becomes plain ignorance. This happened to these arts under the patronage of its idols. In their better moments the Romans themselves were embarrassed by how they had brutalized arts ethereal, and they reluctantly called in those nice Greeks to help civilize the Latin brawn. From this background then, it should be bold but reverent to say that Jesus Christ was nice in truly terrible ways that the bronzed ignorance of Apollo could not possibly be. His primordial innocence gave niceness a fearsome power, even a power to destroy the guilty, as Judas realized when Jesus was even "nice" to him in reply to this kiss of betrayal. Judas threw down his coins in revulsion because he had "betrayed innocent blood" (Mt 27:4).

Christ gave a new power and meaning to the innocent arts. Apollo was god of poetry; Christ stood up as the Lord of the poet on the evidence of David's own poems (Lk 20:42). Apollo was god of music; Christ indicted a whole generation for not dancing to his pipes (Mt 11:17; Lk 7:31). Apollo was god of prophecy; Christ was transfigured while the greatest of prophets hovered like a stunned shadow in his glory (cf. Mk 9:4). Apollo was god of medicine; Christ broadcast through Galilee that "the blind receive their sight and the lame walk, the lepers are cleansed and the deaf hear, and the dead are raised up, and the poor have good news preached to them" (Mt 11:6).

More than a Marvel

There is another contrast, far out of the realm of predictable moral proportions. Heaven does indeed have a language to comment upon it, but it will not be learned in this life, and in the larger life it will hardly be necessary anyway. The monumental difference has to do with plain water. One of the Seven Wonders of the Ancient World was this imitation god at Rhodes gazing out on the horizon of water with commanding face of molten metal, straddling the waves like a man on horseback. In contrast is a grotesque wonder, outside the categories and catalogues of human engineering. It is the true Divine Son straddling a pointed piece of wood on the Cross, that little saddle called a *sedere cruce* designed to prolong the pain by raising the pelvis. Seneca mentions such a device. It only made the criminal look more ridiculous, not like the triumphal hilarity of Apollo, but more like an obscene burlesque all the more hideous when used on a man whose life was grace itself. Apollo's bronze profile with all its grand angles is not on the Cross; there is a skull already battered nearly beyond recognition that painfully moans, "I thirst."

The Seven Wonders of the Ancient World, and all human constructions for that matter, are marvels as spectacles. Christ's wonders are marvels as miracles. A miracle quite literally is that which is *mirus*, wonderful. Not that this exhausts the subject, or ever could. A spectacle can be wonderful too, though it causes wonder by its appearance; a miracle causes wonder just by its appearing. A Colossus, for one example, is more spectacular than an ordinary man; but an unspectacular man walking on water is miraculous. And a spectacle lasts for a length of time, while a miracle just happens. Spectacular statues last longer than spectacular fireworks, but both last longer than the immeasurable moment of a miracle. And a spectacle is not by its nature unique; it can be reproduced with varying degrees of effort. But a miracle happens only once and no two miracles are identical, as no two saints are identical. Twins may become saints, but you cannot make a twin saint; and you can have two miracles, but you cannot duplicate a miracle.

Miracles in Three Types

There are three types within the miraculous; actions above natural order, contrary to natural order and independent of natural order. Christ thirsting on the Cross performed all three kinds of miracles with water. He worked above natural order when he calmed the storm in Galilee. The account, like all these miracles, is simple and iconic in stark outlines. He and the disciples set out in a boat to sail to the other side of the lake. He falls asleep and a storm whips up, filling the boat with water. The sleep of Christ obviously is deeper than normal, and there is nothing to indicate he was pretending. The frightened disciples wake him. He lifts his head and, with a glance, rebukes the wind and the waves, rather imperiously and nonchalantly is the impression, like a teacher frowning for the hyperactive boys in the back row to be quiet. Then he turns solemnly to his own men: "Where is your faith?" The question seems to strike fear in the men as much as the miracle itself, and their focus moves from the miracle to the miracle worker who is so blithely above nature while being so natural. After all, he did not drop down from Olympus to perform this sign; he was wrapped in the most domestic-looking cocoon of sleep, and the disciples had to poke him out of it to do something. "And they were afraid, and they marveled . . . " (Lk 8:22ff.).

Second among miracles are those that contradict nature. These cause the most disquiet among those whose lives contradict nothing but God. A most outrageous example is Christ walking on the water. It is not the sort of sign you can explain away, like saying that his waking at the same moment the storm ceased had been a happy coincidence; or saying he fed the five thousand by motivating the audience to share the sandwiches they were hiding. That kind of rationalizing is slippery with the facts when you are dealing

with the first category of miracles; it is more strained
when it comes to the blatantly contradictory miracles. There
are accounts of scholars in the headier times of liberal
exegesis who suggested that when Christ seemed to be
walking on the water he was really balancing himself on a
stone ledge hidden just below the surface. Perhaps one reason the Infinite Wisdom walked on the water was that he
knew it would annoy liberal exegetes in modern London
and Tübingen. Many have been annoyed by these effervescent contradictions. Some say they lost their faith because
the Church requires them to believe such things. That is like
saying I will lose my mind if I am required to use it.

Contradictory miracles do not take away people's faith;
they take away their composure. Faith may follow, but then
it is faith only in the manner of a disposition. A disposition
does not believe; it is an inclination to believe. True faith,
which is trust, often is actually affirmed when it confronts a
contradiction. But when faith is not formed, a blatant contradiction is disruptive. Christ walking on water is too blatant to explain away; either it happened or it did not. It is
too contradictory to be merely tolerated. If a tolerant Uni-
tarian visitor in a Catholic church sees the Host elevated at
Mass, he may become curious; if he has holy water splashed
at him he may become intolerant. Before Christ gave us the
Sacrifice of the Mass, he gave us the flagrant miracle of the
splashing of the water; and to this day the Asperges precedes
the Sanctus. While the Mass is the world's greatest wonder,
and more than a miracle because it happens more than once,
and thereby may raise the materialist's eyebrows, Christ
walking on water raises the materialist's clenched fist.

The contradictory miracle of the Christ of Galilee also
made an impression different from the affirming spectacle of
the Colossus of Rhodes. The great statue was a very serious
work of engineering that caused as much amusement as

awe. Christ walked on the water with blithe unconcern for any laws of physics, and yet when you expect he would look amusing, he looks more solemn than a man walking to a grave. Instead of causing buoyant smiles, he causes stunned adoration. "And those in the boat worshiped him, saying, 'Truly you are the Son of God'" (Mt 14:33).

A miracle above nature tests faith by stretching it; and so at the calming of the storm the men ask, "Who then is this, that he commands even wind and water, and they obey him?" (Lk 8:25). A miracle contradictory to nature tests faith by shaking it; and so at the sight of Christ on the water the same men cry, "It is a ghost!" (Mt 14:26). A third kind of miracle, one independent of nature, tests faith by shattering it. When at Christ's command an astonishing catch of fish fills the nets, Peter falls at Jesus' knees and cries out, "Depart from me, for I am a sinful man, O Lord" (Lk 5:8).

The first kind of miracle is a sign of God's kingly authority over creatures, banishing storms the ways his popes will banish barbarians; and the response is wonder. But kingly authority is titanism without a prophetic office. The second kind of miracle is a sign of God's prophetic authority against creatures, walking on the water the way his martyrs will walk on human conceits without sinking, and the response is worship. But the prophetic authority is spiritualism without the priestly office. The third kind of miracle is a sign of God's priestly authority through creatures, filling fishermen's nets the way millions of anointed hands will fill millions of chalices; and the response is conviction of sin. Then, and only then, does life become a sacrament.

The entire work of Christ would have evaporated if his deed had been exclusively miraculous. The messianic miracles point to a moral motive and demand a moral response. The Church is founded on a rock, and the rock is not a miracle but the confession of a man. Of course the Church will work God's miracles, but for the most part her biography through the ages will seem humdrum, and critics will pass her off as a failed and tragic human institution. Thousands of altars and thousands of wasted words; thousands of convents and thousands of wasted lives; thousands of books and thousands of wasted brains; thousands of churches and thousands of wasted bricks. And therefore thousands of saints and thousands of wasted passions.

Christ is totally detached from such analysis. His own life was inconspicuous about ten-elevenths of the time, and even then it was of provincial interest. When he says something so common as he says to the men who had fished all night and caught nothing, "*Duc in altum*", Put out into the deep (Lk 5:4), many will think he meant only the depth of water. But he persists nevertheless, bidding men and women to take the plunge with him. And when they do, the humdrum becomes deeper and more glorious than the most spectacular inventions of man. Ordinary habits will turn into habitual graces, ordinary time can become a whole liturgical season, and a meal can transubstantiate into a Mass. When the world is seen from such a depth, it is more than a spectacle. It is itself the skin of God's human face, and the world is not worthy to be so wonderfully worldly.

On the Life of Faith

Here then is the progress of the psychology of faith. It moves from titanism to spiritualism to sacramentalism. Wonder by itself is delectation and, isolated at that stage, the soul is enticed and encouraged by consolations only to become arid and discouraged when they are removed. In the Passion, Herod wanted our Lord to perform wonders. He had no difficulty believing in miracles and even feared at one point that Christ might be John the Baptist raised from the dead, but his decadence consisted in his failure to let humility ferment sensationalism into worship. In this he prefigured the sentimental post-modern type who wants to reject the banalities of modern scepticism while shrinking from substantial credal commitment. He may be edified by Palestrina while avoiding baptism. He may be fascinated by videos of reported apparitions in strange places while rejecting what he calls organized religion. He says "I believe" while putting the accent on the ego instead of the credo. This is the route to superstition.

At the second stage, of formal worship, faith remains incomplete without confession. It has been called cheap grace; in fact it is inflated grace and worthless. Only a deflated ego can make a worthy communion. When lines for confession do not increase as lines for communion increase, a meaningless currency is exchanged for the Precious Blood of Christ. We have been bought at a great price, and we only cheapen ourselves if we do not offer ourselves in exchange. "For what will it profit a man, if he gains the whole world and forfeits his life? Or what shall a man give in exchange for his life?" (Mt 16:26; Mk 8:36–37). God needs nothing that we have; the only offering we can make generously is the offering of our sins with great humility. Peter did not eat the fish Christ gave him until he declared his unworthiness. God wills our confessions. It is the way he prepares us to do his work. As soon as Peter confessed, Christ commissioned him to catch men. "We know that God listens to sinners, but if any one is a worshipper of God and does his will, God listens to him" (Jn 8:31).

Merely affective worship is an action of the subjective desire to be inspired without sacrificing the self. It becomes a spiritual affectation. Pseudo-spirituality of that kind is rampant today, when one is taught to confess, "I do not love myself enough." Before the judging eyes of God, that means I already love myself too much. It is a burlesque of saints confessing that they do not love God enough. When man does not convict himself of sin, when he refuses to accept the consequences of his actions, when he insists that his behavior is not his own, he poses as a victim.

Claiming victim status has become a political industry and a gold mine of litigation. Consider the man who tried to kill himself by jumping in front of a New York subway train and then successfully sued the city because the train had not stopped in time to prevent mutilating him. As the magazines tell it, in the past fifteen years, the number of court verdicts awarding more than a million dollars to persons claiming to be victims of contributory negligence has increased nearly thirty-fold. It is easier to whine about one's addiction than to accuse oneself of vice. Virtually all deviant behavior has come to be called an addiction; there are "sex addicts", "relationship addicts", "gambling addicts", "shopping addicts", and while alcoholism is a disease it now seems that anyone who gets drunk is a victim of his self-inflicted binge. In the immoral modern tragedy, there are numberless victims of social disease; it is considered anti-social to call anyone a spreader of social disease. And there are no more gluttons, for they all have eating disorders. When man habitually complains of victimization, he walks away from the Victim on the Cross, whom man's sins have crucified.

Wonder becomes worship through humility, and through increased humility worship becomes conviction of disobedience. The reverse is also true: the refusal to confess sin (and this includes the refusal to confess sin as Christ orders it to be done in the Church) leads to a refusal to worship, and the refusal to worship leads to a loss of the sense of wonder. Any theorist who thought that the easing of penitential practices would encourage attendance at the Sacrifice of the

Mass was sorely mistaken and should make haste to the closest retirement home for disappointed liturgists. And if anyone thought a sense of wonder would be increased by turning worship into self-congratulation, he need only con- template the glazed eyes staring at the song leader in the sanctuary as he yodels a limp pop ballad into the micro- phone. Empty confessionals empty churches, and empty churches empty the soul of holy awe.

Thirsting as Power

A quick solution for tedium is to create an instant thrill. For a personality influenced more by the right globe of the brain, create a new institute, a radical theology, a new pro- gram, a new scheme for renewal. For left-globe types, it can be a renovation of the sanctuary, a revised Liturgy, or a group encounter. The Colossus of Rhodes diverted many; it saved none. Some of the scribes and Pharisees asked for a marvel from Jesus, who answered: "An evil and adulterous genera- tion seeks for a sign; but no sign shall be given to it except the sign of the prophet Jonah. For as Jonah was three days and three nights in the belly of the whale, so will the Son of man be three days and three nights in the heart of the earth" (Mt 12:38–40).

The one worthwhile anthology of wonder is the Passion. Faith dies without the Cross. The wonder that Christ pro- poses will be his own death. Our deaths are not wondrous; we are refined and coagulated dust but dust nonetheless. His death will be wondrous because he is the one who made us from dust. His last breath will be wondrous because he breathed the first breath into the nostrils of primordial man. It is natural for living beings to die; it is a wonder for the Life of all being to die. His thirst signals the death, and his cracked lips are dying lips. He who calmed the raging waters cries, "I thirst." He who walked on the water cries, "I thirst." He who hauled fish from empty water cries, "I thirst."

Christ's thirst is power. Where men thirst for power, he thirsts as power. And as with all else in the Passion, this is planned. At the Last Supper he denies himself the fourth ceremonial cup, as he denies even the sponge of vinegar on the Cross: "I shall not drink again of the fruit of the vine until that day when I drink it new in the kingdom of God" (Mk 14:25). Drying out and dying out on a bald hill in the heat of high noon is for the conquering of death. In the heat of another noon he had sat at a well in Samaria to tell a suspicious woman: "Every one who drinks of this water will thirst again, but whoever drinks of the water I shall give him will never thirst; the water that I shall give him will become in him a spring of water welling up to eternal life" (Jn 4:13–14).

During one campaign Alexander the Great became much beloved for refusing to drink while his troops were thirsty. And the plain fact is that we are thirsty and do not know it. Christ has water to quench a spiritual thirst so deep that we cannot even feel it when our passions are unmortified. Pilate had that problem, and he thought he was quite in control when he splashed water from a bowl onto the marble floor of the judgment hall as the scourged Nazarene gazed thirstily. But Christ saw a horrible dryness in Pilate that he would die to quench.

Five hundred years before this encounter, and two thousand years before modern encounters, Sophocles said, "I have nothing but contempt for the kind of governor who is afraid, for whatever reason, to follow the course he knows is best for the state." Stagnant water kills, and so does stagnant life, that is, life lived without a regenerated intellect and imagination and will. Stagnant water washed Pilate's hands;

Christ's living water, the power he bestows through his Holy Spirit, could have washed Pilate's soul. With all her earthly limitations and weaknesses, the Church exists for a reason. This is missed when she is expected to be solely a moral teacher and social regulator without the primary function as baptizer of the human race into the death and Resurrection of Christ. "But we have this treasure in earthen vessels, to show that the transcendent power belongs to God and not to us. We are afflicted in every way, but not crushed; perplexed, but not driven to despair; persecuted, but not forsaken; struck down, but not destroyed; always carrying in the body the death of Jesus, so that the life of Jesus may also be manifested in our bodies" (2 Cor 4:7–10).

The owner of a cable television network said a few years ago that Christ had been a failure, and according to this tycoon's standards of success he made a point. More recently he told a convention of humanists that he had come to the conclusion that Christ was "a good man, but hanging on the Cross to wash away our sins? That's weird, man." That probably was the consensus in Jerusalem on Good Friday, too. "Let the Christ, the King of Israel, come down now from the cross, that we may see and believe" (Mk 15:32; Mt 27:42).

Tycoons are not the only ones who say this. It is the taunt of everyone except an occasional figure known as a saint. The world wants a Colossus, not a Christ. Swinburne made elegant his own taunt about "the ghastly glories of saints and dead limbs of gibbeted gods". And this is precisely why Christ thirsts: because we do not. We want to be amazed; we see no need to be saved. But Christ takes our place on the Cross nonetheless to save us. He does what we would not do, forgiving what we do. Affable King Charles II removed his hat when William Penn refused as a matter of religious principle to remove his own; Charles explained to William that court etiquette permits only one head to be covered in the presence of His Majesty. Likewise Christ thirsts for souls when souls do not thirst for him.

Do You Still Not Know Me?

Each of our Lord's miracles is an appeal to faith. None was performed for the sake of the immediate impression. Even the raising of Lazarus, which was done "for the glory of God", occasioned the most dramatic heavenly apostrophe before the public prayers of his Passion. Many of those who were plotting against him and who would witness his death were arrayed at the entrance to the tomb of Lazarus and heard Jesus as he lifted up his eyes: "Father, I thank thee that thou hast sent me. I know that thou hearest me always, but I have said this on account of the people standing by that they may believe that thou didst send me" (Jn 11:41–42).

Many others, however, believed in him from that time. The object of faith is apparent in each of the miracles, but some accept and some do not, because faith requires a free act of the will in response to this act of God's grace. When the marvels of Christ are visible, the intellect can register them, as did the crowd at Bethany; they could see Lazarus come out of the grave with the same clear eyes that could look at a pyramid or a colossus. This is the kind of intellectual perception that Peter Lombard called "unformed faith". Those who "believed", however, were those who did more than see what they saw. Free will provides the option to act upon intellectual perception. Christ prayed that they "may" believe, not that they "will" believe. Fully formed faith is what St. Paul called "faith working through love". He well knew the fickleness of the will: "You were running well; who hindered you from obeying the truth?" (Gal 5:6–7).

The test of faith is the Cross and the aridity of the Cross. The apostles themselves were shaken in the test. For three hours the faith of the apostles was shaken until only the youngest of them had strength, through the virtue of pure love, to withstand the assault. And this is an allegory of our times. When an American generation was moved by its sense of power in the world in the mid-twentieth century, it enjoyed a certain religiosity, even what was called a religious revival, largely based on a sense of cultural pride and contentment. The vast majority of Catholics who had been recent immigrants joined the enthusiasm, satisfied that they had been accepted as social peers in the mighty cultural enterprise. Later this civic faith was shaken when its social supports were challenged, and it moved into a vague and subjective Aquarian spiritualism. Again, Catholics were all too quick to enter into it, especially when misrepresentations of the Second Vatican Council seemed to abolish authentic rubrics and commandments. Even Catholic public figures declared in legislative assemblies and courtrooms that their constitutional obedience to the State took precedence over their moral obedience to the voice of Christ in his Church. When Caesar is stamped on both soul and coin, the soul is rendered and the coin kept.

Among those who were involved with the supernaturally inspired work of the Council, there still are some who find it hard to admit how they humanly misjudged its practical reception and implementation. There are some who think their cherished ideal is real. It is more reassuring for some who invested so much of themselves in it to ignore consequent failures than to admit this ponderous ecclesiastical fact: in practical terms, the Second Vatican Council's address to secularism has been surpassed among the Councils

perhaps only by the Fifth Lateran Council's address to Prot-
estantism in the elusiveness of its goals and the modesty of
its issue. Those who have made Vatican II the proto-typical
and definitive Council will have to be succeeded by a
generation without the same vested interest before a more
balanced critique and measured historical perspective can be
expected. A solid sense of the Christ in history cannot be
learned or taught by anyone who speaks of things pre-
conciliar and postconciliar the way we speak of things B.C.
and A.D. Coleridge wrote: "If men could learn from history,
what lessons it might teach us! But passion and party blind
our eyes, and the light that experience gives us is a lantern
on the stern, which shines only on the waves behind us!"

To the shame of the Church's sons and daughters, impetu-
ous spiritualism and romantic primitivism have appropriated
the Liturgy, which is the chief vehicle of evangelism and
conversion. They have wrapped it in harlequin sentimentality, precisely at the moment when all the world one
way or another is rising from its philosophic comas to look
for substantial truth. Now the Church stands at the turn of
the millennium, trusting that her sacramental life will be
renewed in humble obedience to the Holy Spirit of this
most recent Council and of all the Councils. The various
ideologies that some tried to accommodate are clearly dead
and remain as flotsam on the shaking surface of culture.

The essence of sacramentality is the transfiguration of
creatures by the Holy. The alternative, if one does not
believe in unbelief, is the unformed faith in the self, or "self-
actualization". The psychotherapist Victor Frankl, a genuine
victim of the miserable Nazi stew of titanism and spiritualism, came out of a concentration camp alive to the vacu-
ousness of life lived without God: "Self-actualization is not a
possible aim at all, for the simple reason that the more a man
would strive for it, the more he would miss it." This is what

Christ says through his Church. Legions have taken it to mean that the Church thrives on human misery. But Christ declares with holes in his hands that misery comes from thinking you have everything when you have only creatures. Real misery is represented by the youth with no holes in his hands who in a recent survey listed cable TV as the highest evidence of the American quality of life.

Christ "died for all, that those who live might live no longer for themselves but for him who for their sake died and was raised" (2 Cor 5:15). Shrewd Talleyrand remarked of the counterrevolutionist Bourbons that they had learned nothing and remembered everything. That may describe stunned secularism at the end of the twentieth century, as it quivers with ambiguous memories of the massive atheistic projects that have smothered so many millions in so much misery. Christ says to the age at the end of two millennia of Christian fact as he said to the apostle, "Have I been with you so long, and do you still not know me, Philip? He who has seen me has seen the Father; how can you say 'Show us the Father'?" (Jn 14:9). The words urge formalism to the boldest confession in history: "If for this life only we have hoped in Christ, we are of all men most to be pitied" (1 Cor 15:19).

This is the high noon of Western culture, when it is rightly enjoying the fruits of myriad accomplishments. The greatest parades in human history have recently been winding their way through the streets of the most technically advanced cities in celebration of wars won and a new fraternity among the nations. We are free to build a new Colossus to celebrate delight, but it will sadden us if it has a hard face impervious to the great cruelties and failures in our alleyways and hearts. There is much that some would want to build a civil faith upon, and to them comes a temptation positively to worship the secular order. Or the soul of the nation can turn in its noontime to a figure hanging in an ancient noon, his flesh bronzed and his tongue swollen. "I thirst." I thirst during your parades and conferences and city building. I thirst during your lovemaking and fighting. I thirst during your living and breathing and during your destruction of life and life's breath.

The noonday sun will not pass without a response. Should a hardened society just gaze at him in fascination? Will the sun stay patient if we only worship him as one like ourselves writ large? The sun that shines on skyscrapers and highways also shines on sins. God of the universe and of the seven sacraments waits in this hour to hear a world cry out: "Christ on the Cross! I thirst for you who thirst for me!"

VI

THE TOMB OF MAUSOLUS

"It is finished!"

A Gift of Memory

The sixth wonder was a tomb not quite like the pyramids. The pyramids were built out of duty. The Tomb of Mausolus was built out of love. Mausolus had been a satrap of Caria in the Persian Empire, who died 353 years before Christ. His widow Artemisia, a daughter of Hecatomnus, succeeded him and was a powerful leader in her own right, defeating a revolt of the Rhodians and saving her capital city. The impression is that in the end her emotions got the better of her; the fact is that love got the better of her, which is quite the best thing to get the better of anyone. Her beloved was dead, and so her love took the form of a deep grief, but not an inexpressible grief, for expression of it became one of the Seven Wonders of the World.

By the time she died two years after her husband, and they said then it was clearly death from a broken heart, she left behind the funerary monument for him whose name has become the name of all such monuments since. The Mausoleum. It stood in Halicarnassus in southeast Turkey 135 feet high, rectangular and surmounted by an Ionic colonnade supporting a pyramidal roof, adorned with a frieze and sculptures the work of four of the age's most celebrated artists: Bryaxis, Leochares, Scopas and Timotheus. When the last of their chiseling ceased, and the top had been crowned with figures of the King and Queen in a chariot pulled by four horses, they gazed at a stone fancy like the modern Taj Mahal, and like the Taj Mahal a monument to the remembered.

A memorial is not necessarily a tomb, and a tomb like a pyramid is in fact cloaked in anonymity and is not a memorial at all. But a tomb that is a memorial is the loveliest and saddest of all kinds of buildings and the surest sign that the human psyche is unlike any other creature on earth. As Aristotle taught, and the Fathers like St. Augustine after him, man is an incarnate intellect: he is spiritual, but the lowest in the hierarchy of spiritual beings, and so he needs a body, because his soul is rational, and his senses inform his intellect. Were he pure spirit, it would not be so. But it is so, and it is his limitation and his glory: "Yet thou hast made him little less than God, and dost crown him with glory and honor" (Ps 8:5). Being made in that degree, humans build with stones as do animals, but they build monuments to the soul that no mere animal has.

As a function of the imagination, the memory is a sign of the soul, for the imagination is part of the soul. On a social scale, the memory is a sign of civilization. The imagination is part of the civilizing spirit wherever, in Stevenson's words, "tall memorials catch the dying sun". There can be no civilization where there is no memory. Civilization is the incorporation of a social history, "surrounded by so great a cloud of witnesses" (Heb 12:1). A civilization in isolation suffers a massive social amnesia, and loss of historical consciousness is a loss of radical human consciousness. Evidence today is the near total loss of history in the schools, and many are the greats of culture "who have no memorial, who have perished as though they had not been born" (Sir 44:9). Consciousness of history has become obscure, and where the scientific vocabulary of history remains, it is appropriated for ideological purposes. As the truly great are forgotten, the media perform a kind of theoretical plastic surgery on individuals and events to make them greater than they were, and all to promote an idea rather than to prove a truth.

Memory and the Divine Mercy

Indifference to the past is indifference to God. He is Omega; he also is Alpha. And the Lord of history by various acts of grace revives in the human memory awareness of what he has done from the beginning of time as an assurance of what he will do. Time is a silent puzzle and even a ticking horror without the divine assurance of a reason for it. St. Augustine said that he knew what time is until asked to explain what it is and not altogether helpfully traced its motion from a future that does not exist through a present that is passing to a past that no longer exists. The past is a reference, like the North Star, and we study history to get through life the way we box a compass to get through a forest. Physical science depends on it as much as theology; were there no historical purpose for existence, no Providence indicated by events, there would be no reason to posit hypotheses or to expect conclusions. Modern scientific culture is the endowment of the Christian vision, regardless of how many unbelievers live off the inheritance and spend it in destructive ways.

The fact of the Divine Mercy is an historical fact, and the events of history become a hymn to it. The Blessed Lady makes herself the anthology of all such hymns from the past: "And his mercy is on those who fear him from generation to generation" (Lk 1:50). In antiphonal response, Zechariah, the father of John the Baptist, praises the Lord God of Israel who "spoke by the mouth of his holy prophets from of old . . . to perform the mercy promised to our fathers, and to remember his holy covenant" (Lk 1:70, 72).

God spares the human race because he has a plan for it, and he forgives the past because he intends a future. With the memory of sacred tradition, a terrible cruelty of alienation from God usurps Providence. If we have covered the footsteps of the past, the future is an impossible maze; if man is not part of history, he is an ambiguous incident in time, and if he is an incident, he is an accident. The evolution of the historical awareness of the Divine Mercy may be traced in the progress from Abraham's bargaining on behalf of Sodom. "Wilt thou indeed destroy the righteous with the wicked? Suppose there are fifty righteous within the city; wilt thou then destroy the place and not spare it for the fifty righteous who are in it?" And when he got the Lord to accept a bargaining chip of ten righteous, "the Lord went his way, when he had finished speaking to Abraham; and Abraham returned to his place" (Gen 18:23–33). Abraham asked the Lord twice not to be angry at his request for mercy. By the time of Jonah, the Lord is ordering man not to be angry at the generosity of his mercy. For all the while that man thought he was persuading God, he was being led by the same God to persuade so that he might learn the content of God's salvific plan.

It is the method he uses today with us when sentiment cares more for lower creatures than for humans, and more for private comfort than for the common good: "You pity the plant, for which you did not labor, nor did you make it grow, which came into being in a night and perished in a night. And should I not pity Nineveh, that great city, in which there are more than a hundred and twenty thousand persons who do not know their right hand from their left, and also much cattle?" (Jonah 4:11).

Objects of Mercy

Mercy is in Christ as Christ is in history. On the Cross, in a mysterious way not contradicting his Incarnation, history is in Christ. On the Cross he completes God's historical acts of restoring creatureliness to its purpose. "In him we have redemption through his blood, the forgiveness of our trespasses, according to the riches of his grace which he lavished upon us. For he has made known to us in all wisdom and insight the mystery of his will, according to his purpose which he set forth in Christ as a plan for the fullness of time, to unite all things in him, things in heaven and things on earth" (Eph 1:9–10).

Now salvation is a salvaging of the human condition that has lost its memory of God's plan. God in Christ meets people during his earthly ministry as wandering amnesiacs whom he wants to lead home. To the adulterous woman, rescued from a kangaroo court, he shows a new path with the words, "Neither do I condemn you; go, and do not sin again" (Jn 8:11). To Zacchaeus, with his short legs dangling from the branch of a tree, he calls up a dinner invitation, "For the Son of man came to seek and to save the lost" (Lk 19:10). To Peter in the days after the Resurrection, drying off from a swim and shaking off three betrayals, he says as he said the first day they met: "Follow me" (Jn 21:19).

The person is not a passive agent. His very being depends on his cooperation with God's plan for him, which begins by entering the historical experience of God's creative love. This requires three attributes: goodness, knowledge and similitude. Goodness loves Christ as the way; knowledge loves Christ as the truth; similitude loves Christ as life itself. A soul must seek its good, understand the object of its seeking and become like the object. It is the case to an imperfect degree with love between humans. The world's love songs witness to the joys and sorrows of that human love, and the world's memorials and mausoleums record it for all loves that are yet to be.

Divine grace perfects love so that similitude becomes identity. Similitude in friendship is the quality of liking the same object; in love it is the quality of being the same as the object. Friends are attracted to each other because they are attracted to the same other things; this is the stuff of clubs and societies and lifelong conversations. Lovers are attracted to the same other things because they are attracted to each other; and this is the stuff of faithfulness "in sickness and health for richer for poorer". Friends will go on holiday to the lake because they like the lake; a lover will go to the lake because his beloved likes the lake. "Let's go together" has not half the living grandeur of "where you go I will go, and where you lodge I will lodge; your people shall be my people, and your God my God; where you die I will die, and there will I be buried" (Ruth 1:16–17).

Friends can be rarer than lovers because compatible tastes can be rarer than compatible desires. But love is more demanding than friendship because it requires a sharing of the self rather than a sharing with another. Alexander Pope wrote to Swift: "In every friend we lose a part of ourselves, and the best part." The grief of a lover is of a different order; when the beloved dies, the lover loses the self, and the whole self. In human love, two can "be one flesh", but this is a temporary fact until death (Mt 19:5; Mk 10:8). If there is only human love, its dissolution is an unspeakable sorrow; people really can die of broken hearts like Artemisia.

Human love opens to eternal joy when it is lived as a type of God's perfect and unfailing love. For instance, marriages lived as images of Christ's love for his Church will be faithful and sacrificing, but by being indissoluble they will also be eternal. To say "Catholics can't get divorced" is a stuttering way of saying that love is given and never withdrawn. Of course it is possible to think that love is given by humans, when in fact it is only given to them. It is a deliberate act of God; if you deny that, you lapse into strange and vague language about "falling in love". And in the next breath those who fall in love speak of "falling out of love". It is a strange object, indeed, that we can both fall in and fall out of. It is in fact a fiction. And the Cross of Christ stands as the perpetual sign that love is nothing unless it is what you have to climb up to, through every obstacle that pride puts in the way.

Love will open lovers to great grief if they have not united their own union with Christ. "What therefore God has joined together, let no man put asunder" (Mt 19:6; Mk 10:9). Perfect love "never fails", because it cannot fail. Lovers may fail in trying to love, God does not. And any love that would be "happy" and "meaningful" but not perfect is a contradiction from the start. Love would not exist at all were it not the gift of the perfect One. Love then requires more than goodness; it requires holiness, and a lover who would not be a saint will grow to hate love. And in holy love, after grieving, "God shall wipe away all tears . . ." (Rev 17:17; 21:4).

There cannot be conservative love or liberal love between people. Political categories certainly do not apply to love for God. There is no conservative Catholicism or liberal Catholicism, and if we think such can be, then at most the quality of our love has not gone beyond similitude, and it will end in a shattering sorrow. This is the case whatever talents or energies are spent in the cause of the Gospel. "If I speak in the tongues of men and of angels, but have not love, I am a noisy gong or a clanging cymbal" (1 Cor 13:1). The less Christians seek union with Christ, the more their altruistic energies will make noises and clang in the diocesan newspapers, in parish councils, in rectories, on television talk shows, in homes and wherever the crucified Christ is looked at without an embrace.

Out of the Tombs

In authentic political terms, a careless conservative repeats old mistakes and a careless liberal invents new ones. The animating tradition of Christianity cancels both by uniting with the vital love of God. Tradition then, as the saints have attested, is not a nostalgic human memory of Christ, for that would make the Mass a mere memorial and the Church a mausoleum. The vital love of Christ is repulsed by tombs and he abided in one no more than three days, and even then he was harrowing lovelessness. Whitewashed tombs filled with dead men's bones were for the proud Pharisees and the madmen of Gadara. The sacred tradition of the Church is a remembering in the radically literal sense of *anamnesis*: an undoing of amnesia by bringing the bones back together again alive. It is too literal for the abstractionist, for the effete and the amateur gnostic of the modern age. But it is the way God works. The resurrection of the body according to the plain street Greek of the Gospel is "the sitting up of the corpse", *anastasis nekron*. Nostalgia could not long endure such graphic love, for this love is nothing less than life itself. And the sacred memory of the Church does not transmit so feeble a thing as information about God when it can transmit the life of God himself.

In the sunset of the Day of Resurrection, two men walking on the Emmaus road were sad for Jesus as Artemisia had been for Mausolus, though they could not memorialize their Beloved as she had. The two relied on the fugitive philanthropy of a certain rich man named Nicodemus, who had a tomb hewn and waiting. As the sun sank to the level of their grief, a figure appeared between them: "Why are you sad?" Such a voice of empathetic mercy had never been heard. It had only been intimated in the occasional dialogues of an Abraham or Jonah. Now it spoke with lungs: "What is this conversation which you are holding with each other as you walk?" (Lk 24:17). And they stood still, says the Gospel. They stood still, looking sad. Cannot our age hear it? This voice does not go away. Its acoustics are heaven-high and eternal. Why are you sad, people of the modern cities? Why are you sad, people who learn of life only from newspapers and television? Why are you sad, people who take photographs of yourself to learn who you are? It is not God's will that you should stand still looking sad. And as long as you stand still you will be sad. The Lord of Life does not stand still. He walks along the road and bids you walk with him. This is the sacred tradition: a walk with Christ out of the doldrums and into the light.

Christianity has never constructed a wonder like the Mausoleum, because Christ is not to be found entombed. Two men in dazzling apparel had asked the women at the tomb, "Why do you seek the living among the dead?" (Lk 24:5). And they must ask us now, "Why do you seek existence among the existentialists, and reason among the rationalists, and love among philanderers?" On the Emmaus road Christ declares with the steady timbre of eternity: "O foolish men, and slow of heart to believe all that the prophets have spoken! Was it not necessary that the Christ should suffer these things and enter into his glory?" (Lk 24:25–26). He opens to them the Scriptures beginning with Moses and the prophets and gives back to them their memory, as do the Pope and the bishops with him to each succeeding generation willing to listen. Having done so, our Lord repairs with the two men to a wayside inn where he breaks bread, and in the breaking he is remembered by being the memory. History is in Christ. We do not have to look back to him, and we do not have to look forward to him. He is the Beginning and the End and we have to look into him.

Man the Obstacle

Man forgets God because he cannot forget himself. His egoism becomes a pseudo-tradition. "So for the sake of your tradition you have made void the word of God" (Mt 15:6). Empty grief comes when we look into our own hearts and fabricate a notion of what is in the Sacred Heart. Our hearts have been void since first they were emptied by a lie against life in Paradise. By that lie death came into the world and our ancestors left the Garden to live among tombs. It became such a morbid habit that Christ's own men could not break it. Peter was chief among them. When he tried to stop Christ from going to the Cross and accomplishing the purpose of history, Christ spoke to the Liar lying within Peter: "Get behind me Satan! You are a hindrance to me; for you are not on the side of God, but of men" (Mt 16:23). Satan wants the human race to stand still and to be sad because he is Anti-History.

One theory of why Satan fell from heaven is that he, having the perfect intellect of an angel, knew from before time began that there would be time, and in time God would become a man worshipped by the angels. Satan would not accept this. He would not worship a man though that man were God. He refused to assent to history even before history began, like a child announcing that a particular green vegetable has made him sick before he has tasted it. The first indication of the demonic, said the Angelic Doctor, is that it flies in the face of a known truth. Now that history has begun and is winding its way to a conclusion, Satan's whole purpose in human events is to destroy the purpose of history. He tried it in Eden by making our first innocent ancestors weep. He tried it in Bethlehem by destroying the Holy Innocents. He tried it by keeping Innocence himself away from the Cross of salvation. When we follow the Way of the Cross, the prayers say that Jesus falls three times. The deeper truth is more terrible. He is pushed three times. In a mockery of the Holy Trinity, Satan pushes him to the hard ground through the creatures of Christ's weak muscles and the crossbeam's heavy wood. The deeper truth is also more wonderful, and it is the way the Stations of the Cross may be seen from eternity: Jesus gets up a first time. Jesus gets up a second time. Jesus gets up a third time.

The history of the Church is the record of the same falling and rising. Christ is pushed down by the hostilities and corruptions of false pride, and he rises up in his saints and sweeping reforms. Each time, the Lord speaks through his Church: "I came to cast fire upon the earth; and would that it were already kindled!" (Lk 12:49). The Divine Mercy casts the fire, and we know it is fire because it burns in hearts grown cold. The men on the Emmaus road bore noble witness to this themselves: "Did not our hearts burn within us while he talked to us on the road, while he opened to us the scriptures?" (Lk 24:32). However unique each saint's life is, and however placid or lurid their adventures, they are common proof that God comes to man before man goes to God. God comes with golden intentions for creation, and all the world's rusty grief consists in not accepting that this is so.

God at War

God does not fight little battles. The old phrase could mean either that he does not fight or that he fights great battles. The Emmaus road appearance is the summation of historical experience. Anyone who has lived is by that living fact an historian, and so the one possible conclusion from paying attention to what has been and is going on in the world is that God fights great battles. Of course, this is not easy to see when there are so many miniature struggles to rivet human attention. The neurotic condition of man separated from God confines attention to the little battles: dieting while refusing to fast, fighting air pollution while polluting the body, dreading hardened arteries while oblivious to the hardened heart. As missiles were flying in the Persian Gulf war, a U.S. Army dentist, stationed in Saudi Arabia, told a reporter that the most serious problem facing the troops as he saw it was their refusal to brush their teeth regularly. Great leaders in wartime, as the expression goes, "have vision". Natural experience and virtue may direct vision to the great spiritual battle being fought; sanctifying grace enables the historical consciousness to understand how it is being waged.

An assessment of what is going on in the world requires "being" the will of God in history. This, the state of identity with God's purpose, is conferred by sanctifying grace, the presence of Christ himself in the human soul. Without this grace, the human consciousness of history is trivial and even the most prestigious commentators will make ludicrous forecasts. History is not what we make it, as the Marxist thought; nor is history generally bunk, as Henry Ford thought. History is God at work in the world, and more exactly history is God at war in the world. There have been miserably pious people who were glad to think that God is at war with the world. They have thought that because of little angry battles within themselves. Christ did come not to bring peace but a sword; he gave that sword to people in the world to fight in the world against the Liar who is at war with the world.

Spiritual discouragements against faith have abounded in the last several generations, philosophically and materially. There have also been vindications of faith in God's Providence, and in the latest years they have assumed epic proportions. One symbol is a statue of St. George slaying the dragon, placed in a garden of the United Nations building in 1990, the gift of the Soviet Union. To say the least, such a gift is surprising even now, and it would have been unthinkable a few years ago. Its official title is more astonishing. There was a time when such a figure might have been tolerated as an allegory for "Five Year Plan Defeating Economic Revisionism", or "Worker Conquering the Enemy of the People", or "Sanitation Preventing Disease". The official title is nothing at all like that. It is "Good Defeats Evil".

Who taught the Soviets that? Not many of our own churches have been using such blatant language in recent times. And the answer is simply that historical facts taught the Soviets. To paraphrase Whittaker Chambers, history hit them like a freight train. History is solid and tangible in its stridency. Like St. George and his dragon. There were those who said not long ago that the dragon story was not true, because there are no dragons. While they smiled and looked knowingly over their reading glasses, dragons were breathing fire on nations and devouring the nations' innocent ones. Then they said there are not enough facts about St. George himself. Now we know that the facts are all around us, and they are the facts of life. St. George and the dragon are not a fantasy. There is a foolish assumption, so widespread that it is taken as a truism, and it is this: supernatural realities do not exist because myths are told about them. Now what one means by "real" can vary in context (a clothespin is real in a way a theory is not, but a theory about clothespins is as real as a clothespin); what cannot be questioned is the fact that a myth is only a concept, while God and his saints are not. This is probably why the Gospel books are followed by a Book of Acts and not a Book of Ideas.

History is the mythic term for God's real war in the world. It is no more abstract than the Cross on which God's Son fought his climactic battle. If it were abstract, so then the genocides and ideologies of the twentieth century were abstractions and their victims were phantoms. It has become an affectation to speak of religious truths in terms of "story-telling". What the evangelists call the Gospel of Jesus Christ, some pedants call stories about Jesus. But there are two ways to tell a story; one is to relate an event, and one is to fabricate an event. When a child is punished for "telling a story", he is punished for telling a lie. The stories the Church tells are not of that kind. When she speaks of dragons, she is telling the truth. Victorian explorers thought they had proved that dragons do not exist, and Victorian philosophers knew they had proved that dragons do not exist, but the grand myth of modern history has proved the explorers and philosophers wrong. The full story of the evil dragon has not been written yet, but its plot is already laid out graphically in millions of cemetery plots where lie the carcasses cremated by his fiery breath.

With the possible exception of some of the major newspapers, no voices have surpassed ecclesiastics of a certain naively progressivist stripe in the inane ways they have denied the existence of the dragon. Religion in modern Western culture became a dragon-denying placebo for spiritual headaches. It lost a sense of spiritual combat and sank into two contradictory alternatives: pacifism and terrorism. A curious schizophrenia afflicted religious pacifists recommending guerrilla struggles in territories that fit their political agenda. And this was simply because the spiritual combat of saints and dragons was thought unreal, and political fantasy was thought real. The dominant political fantasy, of course, was Marxism, and it has been found fraudulent like the Wizard of Oz with his smoke and mirrors. The underlying prejudice has just been a lazy optimism about human innocence and the unreality of evil. It was as if the human race fell only in the sense that it was not paying enough attention to where it was going; and that once it got up and dusted itself off, there would be no end to the future. Past and future in fact were said to be infinite. There was no creation; and man had not lost Paradise, he had just gotten out of the primeval slime. According to this theory, man's only obstacle to happiness is man himself. He does not have to be redeemed; he needs a little retooling here and there and soon—Utopia. Of all reveries, this was the most delicate and dangerous; and as man tried to live it as a fact, he found many dragons hiding along the way.

A Most Just War

Man has to face an obstacle harder than his own failure to be good enough. He may not want to call it evil, he may not want even to call it a dragon, but God calls it both, and other names as well. All the names are great and serious, and all God's strategies against this evil are great and serious too. God does not fight little battles. He cannot indulge pacifism, because the war is imminent. There is no hiding place for terrorism, because the war is public. It will be fought as knights in fact and not in fancy fought in pageant on fields of gold with a champion to take the lance on behalf of his lady. A redeemer is a champion, and the world is his field, and the Church is his lady. If the field is littered with graves and the grief of mourning is heard in the land, he rises up to conquer the terrible beast who has brought such sorrow to the kingdom. Should some anthropologist or epistemologist think this a romantic reverie stolen from a bright mediaeval tapestry, let him walk among the ancient mausoleums of man to measure how deep this sorrow is and how surreal this life is without the champion.

> The Son of God goes forth to war,
> A kingly crown to gain;
> His blood-red banner streams afar!
> Who follows in his train?
>
> Who best can drink his cup of woe,
> Triumphant over pain,
> Who patient bears his cross below,
> He follows in his train.
> —REGINALD HEBER

The Apostle Peter, with the best of intentions, wants to stop the war, as he had tried when first Christ announced his intention to go up to Jerusalem. And as the best of intentions can be the worst of strategies, it takes the best man to thwart it. When the soldiers came against Christ in the Garden of Olives, Peter drew his sword only to be rebuked: "Put your sword back into its place; for all who take the sword will perish by the sword." He who comes to send a sword in place of peace has not suddenly become the darling of pacifism. There is a higher and more just war in the wind, and nails will be the swords: "Do you think that I cannot appeal to my father, and he will at once send me more than twelve legions of angels? But how then should the scriptures be fulfilled, that it must be so?" (Mt 26:52–54; Jn 18:11; cf. Mt 10:34).

Four conditions qualify a just war. There must first be a just authority to declare it. Jesus stands before Pilate as a king and declares that the Governor's power is derivative. This he says only after he has spoken as boldly to the Jews: "Truly, truly, I say to you, the hour is coming, and now is, when the dead will hear the voice of the Son of God, and those who hear will live. For as the Father has life in himself, so he has granted the Son also to have life in himself, and has given him authority to execute judgment, because he is the Son of man. Do not marvel at this; for the hour is coming when all who are in the tombs will hear his voice . . ." (Jn 5:26–28).

A just war also has a just cause. Christ confronts the high priest: "If I have spoken wrongly, bear witness to the wrong; but if I have spoken rightly, why do you strike me?" (Jn 18:23). There was no reply except to bind him and send him on to another high priest, true to the type of sullen response when conscious guilt justifies itself by condemning the just. And so Jesus is led away, while his accusers mumble behind drawn curtains about the audacity they fear to look at straight in the eye. Every just war has had such injustice plotting against it at conference tables. Wars fought in the soul are no different.

Just wars have just intentions. And no intention was as noble as the one spoken from the lips of the Nazarene carpenter: "The thief comes only to steal and kill and destroy; I came that they may have life, and have it abundantly" (Jn 10:10).

The fourth criterion is just means. Christ's war against sin and death will be bloodier than any other because it is holier than any other war against any other enemy. False spirituality may be disgusted by so material a proposition, but God is not confined by our definitions of things spiritual. His means of fighting are the definitive expression of justice, and on it the entire doctrine of justification will take shape: "But when Christ appeared as a high priest of the good things that have come, then through the greater and more perfect tent (not made with hands, that is, not of this creation) he entered once for all into the Holy Place, taking not the blood of goats and calves but his own blood, thus securing an eternal redemption" (Heb 9:11–12).

Spiritual pacifism is the subtlest enemy of the soul. Doctors of the soul know it as sloth, the state of indifference to the seriousness of sin and the gloriousness of the universal call to holiness. The slothful soul would rather secure an unjust peace with evil than fight against it. Wherever it is found, and however it is sluggishly lived out, it betrays itself by sadness. Sadness of course is the occasional lot of the fallen human condition, though it is not exclusively that: Christ wept, and the grandeur of heaven was in such moments. His sadness was the constraint of eternal love enduring the afflictions of a transitory world. Lazarus had passed from the scene, and Jerusalem was passing, and this saddened the Cause of our joy. St. Augustine wrote, "If any one thinks it wrong that I thus wept for my mother some small part of an hour—a mother who for many years had wept for me that I might live to thee, O Lord—let him deride me!" But this was not the poor pagan grief of Artemisia for Mausolus or of any noble ancients who had not heard of Christ's own struggle with the grave. Nor was their attachment to memorials and vestiges of the dead anything like the confidence of St. Monica herself to Augustine as she lay dying in a distant land: "Nothing is far from God, neither am I afraid that God will not find my body to raise it with the rest."

In times of peace people may concern themselves with where they will be buried. In times of war people think of where they will die. Christ thought of dying all his earthly life, and his eyes kept looking to the Cross. It did not matter to him how he was treated, so long as he was not prevented from getting there. Oliver Cromwell supposedly said, "Every courtesy to the gallows." No courtesy was shown our most courteous Lord. He was too occupied with his battle to take much note, though along the way he admonished his betrayers and judges and the wailing women. He was out for a fight whose scale they could not begin to measure. He had no debt to pay to society by his execution. What did he have to pay back to his human brothers and sisters? What had the world given him? A swaddling cloth? Some gold and frankincense and myrrh? Some ointment in an alabaster jar? He has no debt to pay to us. He does have a debt to pay for us. The debt of sin factors in the same justice that created the universe according to a harmony. If it should seem small of God to require a payment, then it is small of him to have created the universe.

This is the mystery and motive of his sixth utterance from the Cross: "It is accomplished!" You might translate this, "It is finished", but it would mean what he meant only as the victorious shout at the end of battle. There are tabernacles in churches because of this. Christ has no mausoleum, because he has won on the Cross the war against the cause of grief. His memorial is a live presence, and it is himself. The Holy Sacrifice of the Mass does not need to remember him, when it can re-member him. "This is my body. This is my blood."

The Tomb of Mausolus no longer exists, save for a few fragments in the British Museum. The fact that we can have a memory of the memorial is itself more marvelous than the fabric of the marvel. But even more marvelous are the words cried in a battle for which opaque figures like Mausolus and Artemisia had no idea of fighting, let alone winning: "It is accomplished!"

VII

THE LIGHTHOUSE OF ALEXANDRIA

"Father, into thy hands I commend my spirit."

The Lights Going Out

As the Jerusalem sky darkened over the Cross, a fire was being fueled in Egypt at the top of the Pharos. The Lighthouse, or Pharos, of Alexandria stood on a peninsula of the same name, an island before Alexander developed it, for almost exactly three centuries before the coming of Christ. Its light could be seen for thirty-five miles and guided ships into the most trafficked ancient harbor until that rumbling enemy of the world's wonders, the earthquake, toppled it in 1303.

The major commercial port of the imperial world had recovered from a period of decline largely through the efforts of Ptolemy III. It was altogether fitting, and expected, that some marvel be built to celebrate the renaissance. The Colossus of Rhodes celebrated a new power; the Pharos celebrated a restored power, so it was rather more practical and sober in its design and purpose. The practicality was cautious as well, for, though Egypt boasted, it boasted for self-assurance. For all purposes it had become a vassal state of the Roman Empire and its granaries fed more Romans than Alexandrians. If you asked an Alexandrian, he would tell you that his white marble lighthouse was 600 feet tall. The Romans soberly catalogued it officially at 200 feet. The truth may have been somewhere in between, but the discrepancy tells more about the politics of the time than about its engineering, which in any case was considerable. The

Pharos rose by three sections designed by the architect Sostratos: the bottom a square, the middle an octagon and the top a circle. Rather stolid and geometrical when you think of the almost baroque audacity of the Colossus, it must have been indisputably wonderful to approach from the outer sea. It was at least as conspicuous as "Liberty Enlightening the World", the Statue of Liberty rising in New York Harbor 152 feet tall and 305 feet altogether with its pedestal.

The scale of a civilization may be in the size of its monuments. The fact of civilization is in the light of its monuments. The Pharos held fire and the Statue of Liberty holds electric fire, but in each case the fire is held. Fire does not fall on them or thrash around them; the ability to control a flame is a primal boast of civilization. Fire is light grabbed by time and space; and the heat of fire is the blush of light exposed. Cities advertise themselves by their lights, and Paris laid claim to being the most civilized city as the "City of Lights". No city deliberately calls itself a city of shadows. Only its enemies call it that. As dark streets are dangerous and a symbol of moral decay, a blackout is a failure in a system, both in a city and in a brain.

The story of humans and their hearths is very old. In the 1930s in caves of Choukoutien in northern China, paleontologists found fossil remains of the hunting and tool-making Pithecanthropus. Whatever this has to say about evolution, the evidence clearly pointed to the control of fire half a million years ago. This does not mean that the remains were of humans. Intelligence alone does not guarantee humanity, not any more than the lack of intelligence defeats it. It is one thing to describe Homo Sapiens as a human body with a brain averaging between 1,350 and 1,500 cc., as one standard text does; it is another thing to say that the brain of Homo Sapiens is human because it measures that. If brain capacity defines the human, rather than indicating him, then the crushing of unborn babies and the starving of comatose old people are human acts and anything human is humane. That could also mean that the human race is unwinding. In the shadowy time that called itself the Enlightenment, Louis XVI lost his head on an execution machine named for its inventor, Monsieur Guillotin, whose intelligence the same king had recognized by appointing him along with Benjamin Franklin to a commission for the study of Anton Mesmer's theory of animal magnetism. Intelligent humans cannot become unhuman by devolution; there is, however, a power of savage reason that can dehumanize while posturing as quintessentially humane.

The confidence of some paleontologists was shaken in 1991 by the discovery of a skull in Bordeaux indicating that Neanderthal, from whom they formerly theorized Cro-Magnon had evolved, lived as recently as 36,000 B.C.—a contemporary of Cro-Magnon. The evidence is consistent with the Church's teaching against "polyphyletism". While she is reserved in her critique of evolution theories, since she is first concerned with the Evolver, the Church holds against the picture of the human race evolving from many different branches (phyla) in various areas. One of our newspapers reporting this discovery imagined Neanderthal "poignantly" mimicking Cro-Magnon's gait and advanced use of tools. Here had to be a magnificent example of self-projection. The science editor of that newspaper has the capacity for poignant feelings; but creatures whose confusion suggests poignancy to humans cannot feel wistful in themselves, if such a feeling is the tentativeness between human joy and sorrow, the lip trembling between the smile and the shudder. The noblest creatures beneath man have only grins and snarls, and if I say that the hyena laughs and the mocking bird mocks, I say more about myself than about them.

Was Cro-Magnon, the first known artist, human? If he was, this was not because he had evolved with a higher intelligence. If he was human, he had evolved to the state God ordained to receive a soul. All living creatures have animating spirits; only humans have souls. If this is not so, why does a liberal and positivist newspaper imagine a wistfulness in non-man's glance at man? The impression of poignancy in Neanderthal's imitation of Cro-Magnon is not as sharp as the scene of any one of us today in a state of spiritual tepidity trying to imitate saints by deeds without becoming saints by grace. It is like trying to reach the heavens by a rocket instead of a cross. Then the heavens are black space.

"As sin came into the world through one man . . ." (Rom 5:12), there was a first man in whom spirit and matter were distinct. Original life and original sin require an original man. Both Vatican Councils affirmed the Fourth Lateran Council on this, but the location of the first man becomes totally subjective if you do not boldly "agree" with God that a human is a creature into whom God has deliberately breathed a breath of his own life. The capacity to use fire rather than fear is the inkling of stewardship over the unlit blaze of the unseen light of truth from which life itself is born.

There is still more room for discussing just when the original man was created with a soul, as Paul VI said in 1966 to participants in a symposium on original sin. He moved various glosses on monogenesis into the realm of hypotheses neither accepted nor condemned. But whatever creature was the first man, he received the gift of both the intellect to know God and the will to choose God. So Chesterton says in *Heretics*: "Man can hardly be defined, after the fashion of Carlyle, as an animal who makes tools; ants and beavers and many animals make tools, in the sense that they make an apparatus. Man can be defined as an animal that makes dogmas." Man's biological matter may have evolved, but he was not human until he was directly created man by the endowment of God's image in him. This was a precise gift with potential for maturation but without any need of evolution to be what it is. We may search for a "missing link" between human-like creatures and human beings, remembering of course Chesterton's observation that the only thing we know about the missing link is that it is missing. But should one be found and brought from some hole into the light, it would still be invisible. It would not be other than the mystical love of God saying, "Let us make man in our image, after our likeness . . ." (Gen 1:26). Such is the light that is the life of men.

Pope Pius XII's encyclical *Humani generis* in 1950 said the early chapters of the Bible were written in a "naive, symbolical way of talking, well suited to the understanding of primitive people". It also said that they reveal "certain important truths upon which our eternal salvation depends". If the mind would calculate where the human race came from without establishing where it is going, it would be like a driver guiding himself by looking through the rear-view mirror. The most sophisticated language will not prevent us from crashing into realities that are completely unimpressed by such erudition.

The control of energy does not ensure the humanity of civilization, whose quality is becoming ever more problematic. Pithecanthropus could cook with fire; Pithecanthropus also was a cannibal. When civilization passed from splitting wood to splitting atoms for bigger fires, a possibility arose of "bombing ourselves back to the Stone Age". What that fully would mean is unclear, though it is hardly flattering to the Pithecanthropus family; but at least it admits that the notion of progress cannot be a notion of inevitable progress.

If human civilization is distinguished by the capacity for art, it was imperiled when modern man lost sight of his purpose in God. A dominant kind of modern anatomical art resembled nothing quite so much as that of the Upper Paleolithic culture of only forty to fifty thousand years ago, which practically ignored the face and exaggerated the nursing and reproductive parts of the female anatomy. Scientists use that erogenous usurpation of personality as a sign of incomplete human development; modernists called it self-expression. A dense moral darkness returned to the world just at the time it had modernized its lighting, and cities seemed darkest when neon bubbled and flashed on them. At least some in the cities began to realize the practicality of a philosophical tenet: the control of fire and use of its light civilizes to the extent that humans understand the meaning of light. "The eye is the lamp of the body. So, if your eye is sound, your whole body will be full of light; but if your eye is not sound, your whole body will be full of darkness. If then the light in you is darkness, how great is the darkness!" (Mt 6:22–23).

As the man who said that was hanging on a Cross in Jerusalem, the lighthouse keepers were stoking their fire in Alexandria, totally oblivious to him. Nor could they have attached any significance to the blackening of the sky as he died. There are credible accounts in disinterested annals of an astonishing darkening of the sky across the Mediterranean world reaching as far as Alexandria and Rome itself at that same time, in the fourth year of the two hundred and second Olympiad. Tertullian claimed to have seen archival reports of it, and Phlegon wrote that over Europe stars were seen at mid-day. The augurs thought it an omen of the gods, and those since who have thought themselves free of superstition theorized that it may have been caused by some volcanic ash storm or some such natural phenomenon.

Christ expected a moral darkening, and if it were moral, then creatures would perceive it at least with the "lamp of the body". In the Garden of Olives he told those who had come out against him: "This is your hour, and the power of darkness" (Lk 22:53). As Christ suffered on the Cross from noon to three, "the sun's light failed, and the curtain of the temple was torn in two. Then Jesus, crying with a loud voice, said, 'Father, into thy hands I commit my spirit!' And having said this he breathed his last" (Lk 23:45–46).

At the start of the First World War, when empires wider than any the Ptolemies imagined entered the whirlwinds of their destruction, a specter appeared amidst the phosphorous lights and flashes of the battlefields, stealthily moving behind the noise of brass bands, snuffing out souls and nations. "The lamps are going out all over Europe", said Sir Edward Grey, "we shall not see them lit again in our lifetime." Something more portentous than an occasional world war was happening in Jerusalem, and its Victim was solitary in his knowledge of its meaning. Unwitting human cooperators thought they were in charge. To them it was a legal matter, and the darkening of the sky a coincidence. They anticipated our new slang for violent revenge: "I'll put his lights out." Of course they did exactly that in the physical order of things. And also of course morose Judea stared curiously as the light waned and withered, and the chosen race just sighed like a world-weary woman closing her parasol as some clouds come by.

Light Derivative and Original

In the last six chapters, the word "light" has slipped into the text some sixteen times. Light has a way of slipping in, for life is where light is and light leaves at death, and it acts on words like the white enamelled underpainting that artists from the Sienese school to Maxfield Parrish have used to make pictures luminescent. Each page of the Scriptures glows with the underglaze of the Creator's first recorded words: "And God said, 'Let there be light'; and there was light and God saw that the light was good; and God separated the light from the darkness" (Gen 1:3–4).

A chiaroscuro of light and dark has its violent play in the Passion, light groaning and darkness growling, night cutting into the day. On the Cross it is all different. "God is light and in him is no darkness at all" (1 Jn 1:5). Where the Father is, there is the Son, and where the Father and the Son are, there is the Holy Spirit: the Light of God is on the Cross, even while the human nature of the Son suffers. The Light of God will not be shaded by drugged wine. The Light cannot go out. "And the city has no need of sun or moon to shine upon it, for the glory of God is its light, and its lamp is the Lamb" (Rev 21:23).

Christ emptied himself of this glory when he came to earth, without emptying himself of either divinity or light. He emptied himself of the visibility of that light. Except in the Transfiguration, when it burst out like the sudden ecstasy of a normally discreet guest, it would not be seen by eyes adjusted to lesser lights. "He came to his own home and his own people received him not" (Jn 1:11). This emptying has its own splendor, and the dark shadow of pain crossing his face on the Cross is the lining of a great glory, for the brightness of Christ is its obedience to the will of his Father. The more he suffers the pains of his constricted lungs to breathe out words of obedience, the more all the world's contingent light is attracted to him, so that it drains the sky to be in him: "He reflects the glory of God and bears the very stamp of his nature upholding the universe by his word of power" (Heb 1:3).

The eye can see only those things on which light shines. The light makes them visible, but we cannot see light. Yet we can see Christ, who is the source of light. The light that appears in creation is created, contingent upon the One who lets it be. And therefore the One who lets it be is original light, "begotten not made". He can only be "seen" by love, for love is the power that wills that there be light: "In this the love of God was made manifest among us, that God sent his only begotten Son into the world, so that we might live through him. In this is love, not that we loved God but that he loved us and sent his Son to be the expiation for our sins. Beloved, if God so loved us, we also ought to love one another. No man has ever seen God; if we love one another, God abides in us and his love is perfected in us" (1 Jn 4:9–12).

At the end of the Passion the enfleshment of love closes his eyes, and all is darkness, for the elementary truth is that his eye is the lamp of all creation. "I am the light of the world; he who follows me will not walk in darkness but will have the light of life" (Jn 8:12). He had spoken those words in the treasury of the Temple. You get a sense of claustrophobia when taut voices accuse him in that confined space: "You are bearing witness to yourself, and your witness is not true" (Jn 8:13).

Christ could have made light of their response. Instead he characteristically sheds light on it: "You are from below, I am from above; you are of this world. I am not of this world. . . . When you have lifted up the Son of man, then you will know that I am he, and that I do nothing on my own authority but speak thus as the Father taught me" (Jn 8:23; 28). As he is the source of light, he has no need for human regard to be what he is; he is not a celebrity on whom extraneous light shines, and in fact he passes by unnoticed, as though concealing a great secret. "I have yet many things to say to you, but you cannot bear them now" (Jn 16:12).

The later writings of some of those closest to him, John and Peter, and Paul who was blinded by his light, show that this incandescence has nothing frightening about it in the vulgar and clamorous way of an unpleasant surprise. It is a shimmering "weight of glory" that only hurts because of our weakness, like a matinee sun hurting the eyes when we walk out of a darkened theatre. "For this slight momentary affliction is preparing for us an eternal weight of glory beyond all comparison, because we look not to the things that are seen but to the things that are unseen; for the things that are seen are transient, but the things that are unseen are eternal" (2 Cor 4:17).

When Christ is "lifted up", a mundane expression is turned into one of history's most poignant and wonderful prophecies. He spoke once with the most domestic cadences about lighting a lamp and putting it on a lampstand where it might give light to all the house. With undomesticated screams, he cries out as the nails are pounded into his wrists and the full weight of his glory is hoisted up on the weight of his own nerves. The Light of the World has been put on the Cross, and the prophecy is revealed. The Cross is the lampstand and gives light to the dark-scoured world.

By corollary, this explains the psychology of the tendency of people to take down crosses from their walls when they are guilty. In fainthearted Catholic institutions this has been done frequently of late, sometimes blatantly in exchange for Caesar's coin, sometimes from loss of faith masking itself as pluralism, often as indifferentism pretending to "emphasize the Resurrection", as though Christ rose without wounds. By whatever intentions we operate, consciously or subconsciously, the Prince of Darkness knows what humans in the obscurity of sin learn tragically: to darken society, you do not turn off a light switch, you turn off the Cross.

Light Physical and Moral

The Pharos of Alexandria was a physical light, "whiter than the whitewash on the wall", in the words of a soldiers' song. Christ is a deeper light, his garments "intensely white, as no fuller on earth could bleach them" (Mk 9:3). Civilization needs both. Before the Passover, when Christ was asked the identity of the Son of man who must be crucified, he used physical darkness as a parable for the approaching Passion: "The light is with you for a little longer. Walk while you have the light, lest the darkness overtake you; he who walks in the darkness does not know where he goes. While you have the light, believe in the light, that you may become sons of light" (Jn 12:35–36).

The Lord who made the greater and lesser lights never spurns the physical light as do immoral agents. He even built a little beacon on the shore of Galilee when the disciples were out fishing about a hundred yards off and this was when he had risen from the dead free of all physical constraints. But what drew them to shore was the moral authority of his voice, and only "when they got out on land" did they see the charcoal fire. The scene is a reverse of normal navigation, when sailors see a lighthouse before they hear human voices. And sailors "go out to sea" and come back home; but in the Resurrection, the tossing sea was the bewildered disciples' home until summoned by Christ, and "when they got out on land" (Jn 21:9), their great odyssey began. Physical light guides bodies; but there is a moral light guiding bodies and souls, and it is not ephemeral, because the soul is not ephemeral. When it is neglected, it can frighten. The emperor Hadrian, who liked to dabble in what are remembered as minor poems, wrote of "*animula vagula blandula*"; that is, the "little soul, wandering, pleasant". For him it was "guest and companion of the body". But that kind of flippancy soon becomes a horror, and indeed the great man himself fearfully asked "into what places wilt thou now go, pale, stiff, naked, nor wilt thou play any longer as thou art wont."

If the soul is treated as only a sort of doll in the body, or as Descartes' "ghost in a machine", the body learns the hard way that this is the most deadly of misjudgments. During the Pol Pot horrors in Cambodia, for instance, large numbers of women went "psychosomatically blind" when they were forced to watch the atrocities inflicted on their families by the Khmer Rouge troops. Hysteria has traumatic physical consequences, because the soul has a sight that can be destroyed when the material order traumatizes moral good.

Society cannot be brightened by itself. Dark lies may be taught in the fluorescent light of high-tech classrooms. In cities, zones with the most neon signs tend to locate moral deeds darker than those in the back alleys. Abortion mills use halogen surgical lights the way all-night searchlights marked concentrations camps. The more the human intellect flashes lights in this world, the more the human will can blind itself to the Light of the World. "When it is evening you say, 'It will be fair weather; for the sky is red.' And in the morning, 'It will be stormy today, for the sky is red and threatening.' You know how to interpret the appearance of the sky, but you cannot interpret the signs of the times" (Mt 16:2–3).

As the Light of the World hung on the Cross, sailors sailing into the harbor of Alexandria were cheering the sight of their more plausible lighthouse. At the same time, the thinning crowd outside the Jerusalem wall began to beat their breasts and walk away from the bleak hill. There was no thunder in the sky, but a storm seemed to be gathering. That is how people try to protect their bodies; and that is how souls are shipwrecked. Evil knows only physical light: the high priest's guards and Judas brought torches with them when they went out to capture the Light of the World. Evil fears another kind of brightness visible to the heart. "Blessed are the pure in heart for they shall see God" (Mt 5:8).

By any logic other than the macabre syllogism of Satan in Eden, the opposite is then as true: Cursed are the impure in heart for they shall not see God. By our Lord's own solemn judgment, this is the logic of the moral light against any cooperator with the night: "It would have been better for that man if he had not been born" (Mt 26:24). Creatures cannot will the night, because the night itself is an older creature; but creatures in the image of God, men and women, can will darkness even in the broad light of day as they did on Good Friday at noon. "And this is the judgment, that the light has come into the world, and men loved darkness rather than the light, because their deeds were evil. For everyone who does evil hates the light, and does not come to the light, lest his deeds should be exposed. But he who does what is true comes to the light, that it may be clearly seen that his deeds have been wrought in God" (Jn 3:19–21).

Physical blindness is a condition; moral blindness is a choice. Jesus said of a man blind from birth, "It was not that this man sinned, or his parents. . . ." Then to the pedantic moralists he answered, "If you were blind, you would have no guilt; but now that you say, 'We see', your guilt remains" (Jn 9:3; 41). This is the man whom morally blind men crucified. And the morally blind like them today fling at God the same pompous question that their ancestors thought was the undoing of God: "If God is good, why does he permit evil?" Even St. Thomas Aquinas said it was a most perplexing question, a scandal to the mindful and an agony to the mindless. But he was not blind. He could see the answer on the Cross, and he like all the doctors of the

Church knew that the answer comes as God's question to us: "If you are good, why do you choose evil?"

Four Choices

In four ways a person can choose darkness over light. He can do it first intellectually, like the Sanhedrin, simply because the truth complicates life, as the light reveals more natural curiosities and moral problems than he wants to deal with. He then becomes like the Nazi commander, General Ludendorff: "I repudiate Christianity as not appropriate to the German character." Chesterton replied that it was much as if he were to say, "I deny the existence of the solar system as unsuited to the Chestertonian temperament." If one does not want to bother adjusting to the light, one has this alternative: to follow the countless dismal careers of those who suited themselves to the darkness. By so doing, they insinuated various shades of night into each golden age and bathed in each dark age as if the swirling whirlpool were a lagoon.

This is the position taken by one type of non-Catholic who may with magnanimity of intellect even acknowledge the Church's cultural and social benefactions over the centuries, while remaining a frequent advisor and critic from the sidelines. He will have reasons for doing so, and when pushed to the point the reasons will challenge each other: the Church is too ethereal and too coarse, too exacting and too lax, too vast and too provincial. The Sanhedrin accused Christ from various sides, pulling arguments from their minds like arrows from a quiver. They met more than their match in the mind of the Nazarene: "For John came neither eating nor drinking, and they say, 'He has a demon'; the Son of man came eating and drinking and they say, 'Behold, a glutton and a drunkard, a friend of tax collectors and sinners!' Yet wisdom is justified by her deeds" (Mt 11:18–19; Lk 7:33–35).

The intellect is supposed to reason things out, but nothing could be farther from the intelligentsia's usual way of doing things. The professional intellectual tends to violence more quickly than professional fighters who know the cost of violence. One professor said that faculty disputes are particularly nasty because the stakes are so small. The Sanhedrin would not dirty themselves with crucifying a man; they arranged for others to do it. Ever since, this has been the feline protocol of the cultured despisers of the Church. The Sanhedrin did not refuse to sully their thoughts, however; and when Christ outwitted them, their wittiest riposte was the Cross.

A second way to choose moral darkness is as a flagrant act of the will. This was the method of Pontius Pilate, and it is the economy of modern anti-Catholicism. It is based more on a prejudice than a conviction, and so the cultured tend not even to detect it in themselves. Pilate was frustrated by the obtuseness of the zealous crowds beneath his balcony. Any kind of zeal, save that for personal promotion, was fanatical to his world-weary outlook. For his imperial ego, willfulness was sensible self-assertion in a dog-eat-dog world; zeal for the souls of others was close to lunacy. Christ was a fanatic one way; the crowd was a fanatic another way, and both deserved the contempt of anyone who could not imagine why religion would be something to die for. Pilate's gods were symbols of civic sentiment, and any who took their pantheon seriously, so he thought, were serious candidates for the madhouse. His quick solution was to scourge Jesus brutally in the hope that the bellowing crowd would be satisfied with this near-death and not press for the Cross. Pilate decided for Christ's pathetic innocence but trusted that a lesser evil might obtain a greater good. Only a pragmatist would be so impractical as to trust in an idea that does not work.

Judas became morally blind, not through a defect of the reason or will, but through a defect of the imagination. He anticipated the worst, because he had fantasized his own version of the best, and when his Messiah turned out not to match his imagined Messiah, he had to destroy reality to preserve the illusion. This is the psychosis of the lapsed Catholic who wanders into the night muttering, "I did not leave the Church, the Church left me."

The fourth rejection of the light is purely carnal. Herod was the type of today's lazy Catholics who are repulsed by Christ, not by a reason or a prejudice or a fantasy, but simply by an impulse. As the body instinctively rejects a hostile organism, a body governed by nothing higher than its own gratifications rejects a hostile truth. Herod wanted to be amused. He did not want to be saved from sin, for the only sin in his system was the lack of pleasure. He treated his Savior like a conjuring clown, and Christ and his priests have been dressed that way ever since by red reigns of terror and pastel suburban shopping-mall cultures alike. Herod rejected the Sacrifice of Christ for the same reason the half-hearted Catholic rejects the Sacrifice of the Altar: there is nothing amusing about it.

In these several ways human devices choose darkness over light as acts of autonomy. Dark though it be, it is the self's darkness, and sin would rather that than submit to another's light. Truth requires a movement outside the self, and this is the one human act the human dare not make unaided. From the experience of his own former disobedience, St. Peter wrote to the Church: "First of all you must understand this, that no prophecy of scripture is a matter of one's own interpretation, because no prophecy ever came by the impulse of man, but men moved by the Holy Spirit spoke from God" (2 Pet 1:20–21).

An Ugly Fact

When the General Theory of the Relativity of Matter proved that Newton's theory of absolute space was not absolute, T. H. Huxley said that Einstein "slew a beautiful theory with an ugly fact". So Einstein played an unlikely Samson, but his fact was hardly the jawbone of an ass. The Sanhedrin, Pilate, Judas and Herod each had a theory beautiful to himself for its compactness and universal cogency within the limited universe of his own perception. And they would rather be blind than have their theories shattered by a fact so ugly as a cross.

In an age harsh as his, Cicero called crucifixion the cruelest and most loathsome of sufferings: "*crudelissimum taediumque supplicium*". Its ugliness has slain three theories that beguiled the modern age as effervescent beauties so long as one did not get too close: the superstate, the superman and the superego. The superstate has collapsed in its Communist form and is under severe economic analysis by free-market theorists worldwide, but all its manifestations are under the challenge of Christ: "Man shall not live by bread alone" (Mt 4:4; Lk 4:4). The superman theory has collapsed in its Fascist form, and its vestigial forms of social Darwinism and New Age gnosticism and crass self-boosterism are under indictment: "You shall worship the Lord your God and him only shall you serve" (Mt 4:10; cf. Deut 6:4). The superego has collapsed in its Liberal form. Its angelist anthropology, which denied original sin and assumed the perfectibility of man apart from the life of grace, has been traumatized by the solemn command heard with potency in the forces and events of these recent years: "You shall not tempt the Lord your God" (Mt 4:7; cf. Deut 6:16).

The three theories were flung at our Lord in the defining days of his wilderness temptation, for they are the prototypes of all moral and social mistakes. The third, that of angelism, may well be the root mistake of human meanderings, if only because it so radically misreads the nature of the human condition. Man is not an angel. And when he thinks he is capable of perfection without grace, he becomes a problem to all creation but first of all to himself. In one of the old Nelson Eddy musicals, Jeannette Macdonald is an angel whom he marries, all of which is beguiling until their honeymoon, when her wings get in the way. As a parable of modern moral adventurism, it is what we have learned in countless hapless ways of how sinister false optimism can be, and why Pascal said, "He who plays the angels plays the beast."

Pascal's was a warning contemporary with the attempts of Descartes to construct an angelistic life of the intellect, as if man might know things as pure spirit without a body. It is unlikely that anyone today would be so literally optimistic as to locate the soul in the pineal gland, as he did, directing the body in rational ways like the engineer of a machine. But the many errors to which cultures have since been prey refer one way or another to that graphic optimism: from disregard for free will to the notion that truth is not external but intuitive. The most stifling modern superstitions have been based on this overconfidence in the consciousness of the self.

These are matters for the philosophers, but anyone alive knows that the best-intentioned ideas have brought great misery when they were wrong. The past century has been a conspicuous laboratory for false humanism. According to one story, which if taken seriously still has only the authority of a private revelation, Pope Leo XIII had a vision of the Great Deceiver, who would wreak particular havoc in the world for a hundred years. The intersection of centuries and eternity is a problematic and cautious thing, and intelligent man must be careful in timing predictions. One item needs no caution, because it has been seen in history: the Divine Light came into history and built a little fire on the shore to guide us. The saints have been directed by it through all the ups and downs of the human adventure.

Light Perduring

When our Lord had completed his suffering on the Cross, a struggle he endured to undo the consequences of our self-subjection to the Prince of Darkness, he gave out a great shout that opened tombs: "Father, into thy hands I commit my spirit!" The Churchill of natural virtue said of the Battle of Egypt in the Second World War what is cosmically true of the last breath from the Cross: It was not the end, it was not even the beginning of the end, but it was the end of the beginning. At Christ's shout, the veil of darkness was torn open on the face of creation and the earth shook free of all pretense.

We consider these things from a special vantage point in history. The light of the Pharos in Alexandria, remember, could be seen for thirty-five miles. The Light from the Cross is shining through two thousand years to this moment. Bones of noble souls who fought against the dark in this age, and who by God's grace may now see the Light face to face, are being venerated in lands where they were shrouded by the enemies of God: Beran in Czechoslovakia, Stepinac in Yugoslavia, Wyszynski in Poland and, in Poland too, even Paderewski, who played his music in tribute to a higher harmony. Cardinal Mindszenty's body has been returned to his native land, where enemies of the light had once dressed him as a clown and mocked him as once his Lord had been mocked. In one of those little gestures that the Divine Light sends our way, the earthly remains of this Cardinal, who declared, "The hand of the Lord is on history", are said to have been found incorrupt. "And many bodies of the saints who had fallen asleep were raised, and coming out of the tombs after his resurrection they went into the holy city and appeared to many" (Mt 27:53).

The Wonders of the Ancient World are now old in the way of dust: crumbled stones, fallen towers, sand-swept gardens, darkened lamps. The words of Christ from the Cross are alive and clearer each day. Until heaven teaches a new language, civilized people will have to be content with saying they are the seven wonders of a world that will not end.

"Heaven and earth will pass away, but my words will not pass away" (Mt 34:35; Mk 13:31; Lk 21:33).